COLD SPELL

The View from the End of The Peninsula

Todd R. Nelson

Illustrations by Ariel R. Nelson

Down East Books

CAMDEN, MAINE

Down East Books

Published by Down East Books
An imprint of Globe Pequot
Trade division of The Rowman & Littlefield Publishing Group, Inc.
4501 Forbes Blvd., Ste. 200
Lanham, MD 20706
www.rowman.com
www.downeastbooks.com

Distributed by NATIONAL BOOK NETWORK
Copyright © 2022 by Todd R. Nelson
Illustrations © Ariel R. Nelson

ISBN 978-1-68475-057-3 (cloth)
ISBN 978-1-68475-058-0 (e-book)

♾™ The paper used in this publication meets the minimum requirements of American National Standard for Information Sciences—Permanence of Paper for Printed Library Materials, ANSI/NISO Z39.48-1992.

Cold Spell is for Lesley, Spencer, Hilary, Ariel, Jhonny, and Freya June. It's *our* story. Thank you for sharing the journey. And gratitude to Stoney and Poppa, who found the little town at the end of the peninsula—and to so many inspiring English teachers, neighbors, colleagues, and former students. You're all in here.

*I would really rather feel bad in Maine
than feel good anywhere else.*

—E.B. White

Many of these essays were originally published in *Ellsworth American*, *Castine Patriot*, Maine Public Radio, *Maine Boats, Homes & Harbors*, *Bangor Daily News*, *Maine Times*, *Philadelphia Inquirer*, Creativemainemag.com, *Taproot*, *Christian Science Monitor*, *Wooden Boat*, *Northern Journeys*, *Portland Press Herald* and, of course, the *Adams School Weekly Newsletter*.

Contents

Contents

Contents

Autumn

CONTENTS

A Note to the Reader

Once in everyone's life there is apt to be a period when he is truly awake, instead of half asleep. I think of those first five years in Maine as the time when this happened to me . . . I was suddenly seeing, feeling, and listening as a child sees, feels, and listens. It was one of those rare interludes that can never be repeated, a time of enchantment. I am fortunate indeed to have had the chance to get some of it down on paper.

—E.B. White
One Man's Meat

E.B. WHITE SPEAKS for me. Maine speaks to me too. In my case, the Maine enchantment began long before we lived here. It was an enchantment that we intuited *would* be here, and we had to give it a try.

We were living in Chicago, at the time, and wondered, *What would we be like as small-town people?* Was this our calling, to live in Castine, the small town at the end of a peninsula on Penobscot Bay where we had been spending summers since our kids were little? We needed to answer that question. It would be at least a one-year sabbatical from our metropolitan lives, or it would be

. . . what? The rest of our lives? We're still here. Have you lived here your whole life? Not yet, says the Maine wit.

We made the move. We had no jobs, only a house to land in, our three kids at vulnerable ages, but willing to try full-time life in the land of their summer vacations. What lucky fools. It turned into a family epoch of wonderful activity, professional and personal development, an unlimited source of writing inspiration, hard work and struggle, friendship and, yes, "enchantment." The Maine we expected to find was here. Were we the people we expected to be? That's still evolving. We are still detecting what Maine reveals about us, what Maine has done to us.

For me, around every corner there has been something new to write about. This collection is about rounding those corners with curiosity and surprise. It is a chronicle of seeing, listening, and feeling as never before; having new senses for a landscape and its denizens; understanding the interplay of resources, rights, and responsibilities in small-town relations; of the minutiae of the intertidal zones of the coast and its human communities. And it eventually included six years as principal of the Adams School in Castine, represented here by several essays from my weekly school newsletters. That experience alone made me a columnist.

I'm fond of citing the larger family arc behind these stories. My great-great-grandfather, Spencer Colby, descended from the early Holden, Colby, and Churchill family settlers of Moose River, Maine, the area on the Canada Road around Jackman. He was a farmer and blacksmith, fought in the Civil War in the 14th Maine Regiment (I have his Civil War correspondence), and then decided to go west to Michigan in a covered wagon with his wife Josephine Churchill and eight children. They were in search of better farmland—fewer rocks—no doubt. They had more children in Michigan, then kept going, to Marquette,

Nebraska, where they are buried in Richland Cemetery. You can find them in this book.

Sometimes it feels like my life arc is a grand return to the Maine starting line. I do not earn my living by manual labor, but I am inspired in a romantic way by a few rural skills I've acquired in our rural Maine years. No, I am a scribbler. But I hope a few of the observations that I've hammered out will honor all the ancestors whose lives resonate in our migrations and pilgrimage back to the family headwaters. Here are my observations of the seasons, the critters, the neighbors, the land itself, the jobs and the community we joined that has made this such a rewarding place to call home. And, between the lines, a considerable amount of myself.

I thought long and hard about collecting these essays into sections. They were written over many years, one at a time, and there could be a rough chronological pattern in which they cohere. They could be gathered according to themes like The Village, The Harbor, The Forest, The Denizens. And Paul Manning. After a career as an engineer on oil tankers, Manning came home to work in recycling, town government, and scientific analysis of quotidian experience. He is in these pages. See Manning's Frozen Confection Coefficient, small boat surveying, and clothesline thermodynamics. Manning has been a guide and inspiration for coping with the pleasures of life lived at the speed of intertidal ebb and flow and the afternoon creep of Elm shade.

Most people have an organic sense of seasonal themes in their own life. So be it. Let us follow the footsteps of life lived according to seasonal ebb and flow. And let us begin in winter.

My title, *Cold Spell*? The first essay has always been a favorite. And as I think about it, Mainers live in relation to cold, whatever the actual season. It is always winter or the anticipation of winter, or the memory of winter in this regard. Even the summer people on leave from warmer climes dip their toes in the icy anticipation current and try to imagine what a Maine winter must be like, as they paddle unfrozen water or enjoy a summer fire in the fireplace on a damp, foggy, August morning Down East. This is where winter goes for the summer. We are either preparing for it or recovering from it, and always talking about it. Summer, spring and fall are not independent seasons—they are respites or preparation for *cold*. Everything in Maine life is *sequelae* of cold. And it casts a spell. It is a source of pride and complaint, pleasure and pain, hibernation and exuberant embrace. It is always out there, watching and waiting for its chance to return. It is why summer is the shortest section of this book. Check your wood supply and pantry. Finish the canning. Clean the chimney. We are done with the cold when it says so—not before. Anticipation is all. Let's start there.

—Todd R. Nelson

Winter

Cold Spell

EVEN THE DOGS WON'T GO OUTSIDE. Gus, our big black retriever, will at least tentatively point his nose into the wind on the back porch and give a sniff, but little brown Ivy just turns tail and trots back to the sofa by the woodstove.

The thermometer says it is cold enough to require new language for cold. The television weather commentators are scrambling for new metaphors. The old figures of speech are too warm. We are in a metaphor inversion: it is burning cold.

It's also time to complain about the roads, now that the cold is heaving the tarmac at the usual culverts, with a few new spots thrown in for good measure. The ride to work is a thirty-mile endurance test of front-end jouncing and obstacle alerts. It's worse being a passenger. "Watch out!" I cry, as my daughter navigates the Western County road to school, and we brace and catch our breath for another hard bump to the undercarriage along this minefield.

Nonetheless, I love this arctic spell. The fir trees crackle, the walk to the car is crunchy underfoot, and puffs of powdery snow explode off the stone walls as they are gusted by rogue winds. I'll stand out front by the firewood chopping block and suck in hard just to feel my nostrils clinch and the air singe my cheeks. The moon will be full tonight, and the cedars will do an eerie shadow dance on the alabaster fields at midnight. Back on the knoll, deep in the woods, two o'clock in the morning will feel like a Taj Mahal of cold, white, domed silence.

It used to get much, much colder here. There are men and women living on this peninsula in Penobscot Bay who remember when the saltwater froze over and you could drive a car from Castine to Belfast—seven miles across the ice, versus thirty-five miles via the Waldo County bridge. Now that must have been cold. This week's slushy ice floe in Smith Cove, across from Eaton's boatyard—even Kenny Eaton couldn't remember ever having seen that—still pales by comparison.

The fact that the bay hasn't frozen in a great-grandfather's while is a bit troubling, considering the portents of global warming. To think that so much climatic change could have occurred within living memory! In Castine, cold used to be a business. Don Colson, the local newscaster, remembers when his father cut blocks of ice out of the town reservoirs and slid them down Main Street to the icehouse. That means we're one generation away from original refrigeration.

In the age of sail, Castine ice went to the Caribbean, China, and India. Castine ice made the rajah's sherbet. Castine exported the very concept of cold when it sent ice to the tropics. Cold was a valuable commodity, and we were blessed with an abundant, free supply.

We've gotten soft. Aside from the loss of an ice livelihood, we don't have to struggle against the elements. We don't break the ice on the well with an ax, or haul water to the horses. We don't have to keep the kindling box full lest the cold get the better of us in the night—the furnace will kick in, after all—although I will need to haul a few more trees out of the woods tomorrow and replenish the log pile on the porch. That's as close to free as a BTU can get.

Our cold spell has made a certain kind of harvest possible: lumber. I've waited for the ground to freeze this hard before driving my tractor over it to skid trees out to the field where I can cut them and split them for firewood. My field tires will make tracks in the snow, but by spring there will be little trace of this mechanized incursion. Robert Frost said, "In winter in the woods against the trees I go." The depth of this frost in the ground allows me to tread lightly. If the tractor will start, that is.

And as hard and lifeless as it seems at the surface, I know that not too many inches below the snow things are moving. There is always a layer of activity down in the dark soil, below the frost. From their nests deep beneath my log piles, or among the tree roots, moles and mice surface to a seed stash—we see their tracks skittering across the leach field—the unwary potential prey of cats, hawks, foxes, or coyotes. And water still moves sideways through the earth, as our sump pump indicates when it whirs every so often to keep the foundation dry.

Skunks and owls are mating; the does browsing our cedars are slow and heavy with spring fawns and drag their hind legs in the deep drifts. Most significantly, catalogs arrive in the mail tantalizing us torpid gardeners with beefy tomatoes, strawberry plants, or monster pumpkins. And my mind turns to the lupine seeds I scattered about the field and clearings last fall. Without a hard freeze we won't have new flowers! Yes, it's *good* and cold, auguring robust purple flowers in July.

Having a Mind of Winter

THIRD-GRADER PHOEBE was moseying her way back into the schoolhouse at the end of recess. "I like to listen to the ground," she said, coming through the door. "The ground tells you stories."

Now that was an unusual excuse for eking out a few more minutes on the playground. But I knew what she meant. Perhaps it's the austereness of sound in winter, or the fact that there are simply fewer things *to* hear, that heightens the rewards of paying attention with that particular sense. Then there is just the stark clarity of sound, and its absence, in our zero-degree weather. We are accustomed to the range of sounds emanating from up high—wind in branches, sleet on the windowpane, the occasional crack of frost in a fir tree—but Phoebe was listening down low. She had her ear to the ground. She was right: it does tell stories. Winter sounds different—that's where the stories are.

Fifty years ago, I spent my third-grade free time on Mr. Hurley's pond. It was the neighborhood rafting mud pond in summer and the skating rink for us kids on winter afternoons. But whenever the hockey game petered out due to cold or calls to "come for dinner," or we tired of skating in circles to practice our left and right turns, we would slump down on the ice in our snow pants and crawl around, herding up like seals on an ice floe inspecting its air bubbles, fissures, and trapped sticks and plants—even the occasional frozen minnow. Eventually, we would cease moving and just lie there, listening, as the cold seeped through our insulating layers. There is nothing like listening to pond ice, on pond ice, as a seal. Such cold is dead calm.

At first, when you put your ear down to the frozen water, you hear only your own breathing and heartbeat. Then, as you relax and embrace the cold, the pond begins to speak. The ice telegraphs even minute skate-stomps and glissades from rim to rim, and the rare popping of the release of its own surface tension. Eventually, I swear, you can hear the sound of frogs sleeping. Or the summer story of a spring-fed childhood pond. You stop caring how wet your mittens are or how cold your toes are becoming. It's worth it to be this still and to hear something this noiseless . . . to be in the soul, the "Epipsychidion," of cold. Do not, however, succumb to the temptation to touch your tongue to the pond surface. Everyone knows how that ends.

John McPhee writes of once when, canoeing a Maine stream and hoping for a moose sighting, experiencing "the stillness of a moose intending to appear." On Hurley's pond, lo these many years ago, I knew the stillness of ice intending to melt. It is a sensation, felt not seen. But what have we *but* our senses to describe external conditions? When released, our inner senses—of memory, relaxation, of authentic blissful languor—take us to wholly other realms. It is an equilibrium we achieve, between being pulled forward or back, out or in, home or fifteen more minutes of tranquility unlike any other—like the pivotal moment between water freezing and unfreezing. It's the moment we will await all spring—the ice jam of memory releases the logs for the river drive downstream to summer.

Then, after the ice does finally melt, the pond migrates back to liquefaction. We will enjoy another atmospheric phenomenon: holding your breath under water, resting mid-buoyancy, your heart beating in your ears, aching to inhale but holding out for a few final seconds to savor suspension from all sound and sense. On a hot summer day, we will squeeze the last farthing of oxygen from our bloodstream to linger among the amphibians, *as* an amphibian. Remember that fleeting serenity, just before the panic to inhale? It is the polar opposite of ice serenity, and yet a familiar sonic realm.

Wallace Stevens knew this deep inner listening. He wrote that, like the snowman, "one must have a mind of winter" to "[behold] nothing that is not there and the nothing that is." Have a listen. Put your ear to the frozen ground, as Phoebe did. Let that "mind of winter" be in you. It'll talk to you. It's an old story—it's *your* story. So, get ready. It'll be here soon. The mind of summer will follow, all in good time. Hear it?

Embers

I PLAY A LITTLE GAME when I'm forced to abandon my warm bed on a late winter morning, the house still midnight-moonlight-cold. I tender a touch to the top of the woodstove checking for a vestige of heat, and then gingerly open the door, letting the draft subside. I'm hoping for an easy restart. We're at the bottom of the nightly cooling cycle, and ready to revive the house. It'll be the first of many times I minister to the fire in the coming day, stoking, stirring, and snugging the fresh logs. Fires love minding, and woodsmen love to give them attention. My fire needs me, and I need my fire . . . at least for a few more weeks.

Today there's no hint of flame, but as I touch the iron stove top, I detect a faint persistence of heat. I plow the ashes and rattle the grate, rousting embers like I'm gleaning glowing spuds. If there is even a kernel of fire, there is a chance of today's fire being the heir of yesterday's, and yesterday's the day before. If I can rekindle a blaze from this one little ember, I win and keep the succession alive. I fetch some cedar kindling and replenish the wood box.

According to legend, there are peat fires in Scottish crofts, "the old country" to our family, that have been continuously burning for generations, given just such care—a lineage of warmed hearth and happy kith and kin. The new day's fire produces embers from which to kindle tomorrow's fire, like mine. Not the end of this fire, it's the beginning of the next one: coals as one fire's moraine on which to scaffold sticks, then logs, then introduce the chimney draft which needs only a little heat to respire.

Yes! An ember endures. No match required. Flames rise to ignite the paper and twigs, then logs, and soon a roar of air mixes with fuel, an inhaling rush auguring warmth. Wood journeys ember-ward. I win, again. The house stirs. The dogs draw nigh. The flue murmurs in low octave like a pipe organ's bass notes.

It's like the proverbial sourdough starter—alchemy of bacteria meeting water and flour. It could survive earthquake, wind, and fire in San Francisco to deliver today's famed bread. Though not literally the original ingredients, an attenuated heir imbues the modern starter with at least spiritual molecules. Each day it must be fed and cared for, extending the lineage of baguette and miche, pain de famille, or ciabatta. It was a traveling ember of leaven, something that could journey by covered wagon on rutted roads, and from San Francisco goldminers and their unique bacteria (*L. sanfranciscensis*) to raising up a new metropolis of boutique bread. But sour dough is older than that—perhaps the Ur leaven, from the Middle East, first cousin of brewing and ember of any day's bread, or beer.

A similar leaven is at work in my spring fields. When I walk to the mailbox, I check what's stirring among the dead leaves and winter debris. In the old cow pasture out front, there are lupines that fling their seeds abroad each summer. They've spent the winter hard frozen in the ground and now, if their husk can crack, will start to sprout, root and bloom. I nurture hope for these offspring emblazoning my view from the porch by June, then flinging their seeds askance come August. Radiant colors; new fire from old; a gift from winter storage.

The true Ur ember, of course, is love. It can be hard and resistant to kindle—sometimes husk-shielded by chance or intent—and yet more enduring and persistent than any other human fire when fueled and put in the proper heart's draft. Love warms the house and bakes the bread, cuts the bouquet for a romantic vase or rewards the gaze with springtide blossoms. It swaddles and comforts and gently inspires care and feeding of the whole family, hearts and hearths.

How much we are the fires we tend—the bread we bake, the gardens we plant along our paths, the love we nurture and share. How much tending they take, but what warmth, what nourishment; what joy they bring, and give, and preserve for the next day, and the day after that—generations, like those Scottish fires, if we have a care for the diminutive ember.

The January
Woodpile

IF YOU'RE ANYTHING LIKE ME, and your winter is proceeding anything like mine, the woodpile is a kind of barometer. The forecast is looking good.

It's been somewhat warm, despite a few short, arctic blasts. The January thaw is expected this week. And one can begin to feel that the woodpile will hold out for as long as it needs to hold out, that back in the summer, I managed to cut and split and stash away sufficient fuel. Relief. *Going to make it,* I think. There's still February, I know. And March hill. But the rate of fuel draw-down is working hand in hand with time and temperature. I am like a squirrel that's keeping an eye on the acorn stash.

As a teacher, I can't help but think of the school year as a bit like a woodpile. It started in September with 175 school days, stacked up tidily like so many logs, to be drawn down hand-in-hand, with time and learning temperature. That's right, learning makes heat. As of this week, we've burned through about half of the pile. Middle Day will be around January 27, right around lunchtime, pending snow days. I always feel the tipping as we summit and then shift over to the "Western slope" of the school year. Our watershed will then run toward the Pacific of summer, and we gently descend to summary accomplishments and finales. We will have fully inhabited, say, "fourth graderness" and can start to anticipate the next year.

But, unlike a woodstove, learning burns at an unpredictable rate and temperature. There's more heat in the second half of the learning log pile than in the first half. And there's always a bit of spontaneous combustion somewhere in the year. You just never know when a smoldering coal is going to ignite and flare up. That's the kind of school day we live for.

Back to February. Yes, we can grow the pile by adding more days if we lose some time to snow. It's like the proverbial glass that's half full . . . or half empty. Are we building up or drawing down? Both.

Or let's throw out the metaphor because it's so confining. We're always adding up *and* counting down something, if you look at life in linear terms. But there are so many other variables at work besides time and wood supply. Like the path we're taking on the next part of the hike. Are you seeing those planets in the morning sky? Are you starting to envision wild berries blooming in the field? Bird migration? Open water fishing isn't too far off. And when will "ice-out" be this year? Anticipation is its own kind of slow burn.

Predator, Prey

AFTER BREAKFAST ON SATURDAY, a day that was a sunny respite between storms, I looked out to the dooryard. There on the snow beneath my friend's bird feeder was an exquisite seasonal etching: broad wings, like a snow angel, imprinted in a perfect circle, and a deep talon thrust crater in the center.

Evidently, an owl had seized dinner (a red squirrel, mole, or mouse scrounging birdseed?) and left its impression. Angel indeed. This was a murder scene—or feast, according to the beholder. The snow recorded the gossamer brush of feathers, the piercing plunge of a raptor's feet, and sudden extraction of the hapless wee mammal. An owl swoops soundlessly, its feathers making zero acoustic ruffling as it strikes—sudden death from above.

It seemed the perfect figure for where we are and how we feel in the final week of February in a hard, challenging winter. It made me think that in this winter of intense, lingering arctic air and dense snowpack, our lives too are depicted by this predator-prey drama. Sometimes we are the ruthless barred owl; sometimes we are the hapless mouse.

Another winter storm swoops and feeds on us, as we tunnel beneath the snowpack, scurrying between our storehouses and nests. Or we ourselves are the owl, biding our time to hunt, diving from above to grab the morsels of nutrient we seek, then retreating to the nest and feed. Only, at this point, our morsels are a break from shoveling, adding a little more light each day, coffee and baked goods—a respite from life in this harsh latitude. But a day like this also makes us feel like we just might be on the glide path to something else—swooping downward to spring, on extended wings, from our high perch above the ice and snow.

Waiting for Ice

AT SCHOOL THIS YEAR, we managed to get the jump on Old Man Winter. Before the ground had frozen, before the first snowfall, before the first night of pond-freezing temperatures, Dave Gelinas installed the special rink brackets and side boards in place on the yard out back of the school. Dave is a 5th-grade parent. We call him the Rinkmeister. Our thirty-by-fifty-five-foot rink was ready for water and, hopefully, ice. An empty outdoor rink awaiting water is a hopeful sight. It had everyone practicing lacing their skates.

Ice is always level, of course, but last winter the ground beneath our ice was not. So, this story actually begins in August, when Skip Farnham had his excavator in town digging a trench at the library. With heavy equipment lurking so close to our sloping playground rink, how could we *not* try and level it? The "deep end" would be gone, and it would require much less water to fill. It might even freeze faster?

The 5th graders had already conducted a measurement exercise, using their counting wheel, to determine the area of this year's rink. Once the water was installed, they could work on calculating the volume of ice. Water does a better job than Skip's laser transom at finding level, though it's hard to beat his sure hand on the pneumatic controls while pushing twenty cubic yards of topsoil into the problem corners. Who knew there was so much math potential in creating a little skating rink?

How fitting that it was the day we reached the section in *A Child's Christmas in Wales* with the episode of Mrs. Prothero and the Firemen. Where would our skating rink be without the Volunteer Fire Department, always eager for an excuse to get Engine 6 out for a practice run. Ice water is but a phone call away.

"Call the fire brigade," cried Mrs. Prothero as she beat the gong.

"Call Tom Gutow," said our kids.

I did. "Tom, any chance you can make a water delivery this afternoon?"

"I'll make a few calls and see what I can do," said Captain Gutow.

Meanwhile, the word at school had gone out that the fire department would be coming. "Are they here yet?" asked the kids, every ten minutes, watching out the classroom window. Several of them even stayed after school hoping to watch the big red truck disgorge the flowing future ice.

By 2:30, Miles and Aaron had appeared at the school with Rescue One, Engine 6, and a few other fire department trainees, to scope out the improvements. We assumed the "Guys Looking at a Construction Site" posture—hands in pockets, grouped around the rink/trench in Main Street/foundation hole perimeter—sizing up the situation.

I explained our leveling project, the new support brackets, and the pristine liner awaiting a few thousand gallons to weight it down and, hopefully, freeze.

"We'll be back in a little bit," said the leader of the local brigade.

By 3:30, the fire department was back and pouring water into our rink. Within minutes, 1,200 gallons had flowed onto the plastic liner. The corners and sides were holding. The firemen went to fill up again and return with another dose. After another 1,000 gallons, the whole plastic liner had submerged. We were in the skating business—almost. Cold permitting.

The temperature was not as cold as we would have liked—we needed old-time cold, frozen harbor cold—but at least the rink passed its first test. There were no apparent leaks. The surface may be pocked and slushy, but it's a great start. By the next morning, a few pinecones had fallen into center ice—par for the course, it seems.

Now we can dream of new games at recess as we watch the thermometer expectantly and listen to the forecast. A dozen brand new, red-handled brooms await the first game of broom hockey, and one-gallon plastic milk jugs are being readied as curling "stones."

Now if only the iceman would cometh. Unfortunately, as of yesterday at noon, the 7th graders found several frogs swimming around the edge where there should be ice. Apparently, the local wood frogs think it's a swimming pool, not a rink. I'm afraid it is. Old Man Winter is not playing fair with us. Penalty box. This *is* Maine, right?

Enough Is Enough

February second, Candlemas day:
half your wood, and half your hay.

Half the winter has passed away,
we'll eat our supper by the light of day!

THE CHRISTMAS DECORATIONS have been down a while—a melancholy ritual, reclaiming the living room—and the dooryard looks forlorn minus the glowing snow globe inflated by a fan. The evergreen garland on the mantle is brittle and sere. It's gotta go too. Our Christmas tree has been out back on the leach field for a while, attracting woodland foragers. Forget the customary presentation of the groundhog and his shadow test—according to the old adage, on February 2, Candlemas Day, it's all about the pantry.

It's about whether we will have *enough*. Here on the seasonal continental divide, you look down the western slope and wonder if you have sufficient resources to reach the coast of spring. There'll be no more harvesting. Did you stockpile sufficient firewood? Will the livestock have their hay? The moment is about anticipation, and about our concept of "enough."

We are halfway. Wood and hay are the traditional benchmarks of a former time: practical, agrarian, and fundamental to the survival of the farmer and his livestock in the northern hemisphere. Wood and hay are harvested and stored in advance of the season of need. However, even we non-farmers should assess the pantry. Have we stored fuel enough to keep warm and fed through winter's second act? How's that gauge on the oil tank looking, down in the basement, to say nothing of this week's price of #2 fuel oil? What other kinds of fuel and food are we drawing down?

I find collateral meaning in "warm and fed" cold days. The farmer's entire adage applies literally to only a few of us. No, my wood stove will not go hungry. Yes, half the wood box is empty… however, half is full. Looks like the mice will also have enough. They're enjoying life mid-level amidst my logs, as revealed by their half-gnawed acorns, discovered as I bring wood indoors. Their nests of shredded grass hold fast too. I hope they haven't infiltrated my cozy domain. I like boundaries.

My imaginary horses and ruminant cows graze comfortably on food for thought. There's always enough. But I do take inventory of my actual larder and last summer's hand-picked frozen blueberries. Am I sufficiently stocked to make it to ice-out, or whatever you use as the boundary of winter and starting line of incoming spring? Blueberries are my solar energy of choice, a concentrated nugget of August sunny days preserved in jars or freezer bags, like amethysts in amber, awaiting measured doling of cold weather comfort in pies, pancakes, and muffins. By the wood stove, naturally. Enough? Yet to be determined. One critter's acorn stash is another's blueberries is another's hay. Factor in appetite and critter size.

And how far will the leftover turkey soup and chili from Thanksgiving last? Not too much farther, hopefully. Enough.

These are just the literal provisions. Consider the figurative pantry we're building up and spending down, as we inhabit the season of foresight and hindsight—and test both. We look backward toward supply, and forward toward use and resupply, an equation that must balance. The solution is simply *enough,* and it's a moving target.

Winter draws us inside, the season with sharp lines of demarcation between inner and outer, of closed windows—the season of torpor and hibernation and contemplative restoration, of longing and observing, watching that frozen outer landscape for signs of the wane of cold and snow, of ice-out, of buds and returning songbirds.

So, we are halfway through the work of our hibernation, watching our inner, emotional pantries. While keeping warm, and sharing all that hay, literal or figurative, with our "livestock," we've been doing something restorative. What are the wood and blueberries of our inner lives? To each his own. A cord or two of books will do for me. One man's woodpile is another's neglected reading pile, or yarn store.

Yes, spring and summer will come in good time—it's a certainty thanks to celestial mechanics—and the resumption of wood and hay harvesting and stockpiling for next winter's supplies. The sun is on its way back north where it will warm the blueberry barrens too, and the next annual ring on our next Christmas tree. But for now, we throw another log on the fire and mix another batch of muffins, sip tea with satisfaction and longing, and count the added minutes of sunlight this week. The reading pile is still casting a long shadow, I'm afraid. Enough said.

Snow Day Owl

HE APPEARED WITH THE FIRST FLAKES of the impending snow, swooping in low out of the woods and into our field. He took up sentinel duty on an 8-foot-tall fence post by the garden. From a distance, he looked like a huge ball of yarn, or a post with a woolly hat on top. He shifted from foot to foot, his head swiveling in its fuzzy gimbals to stare at the man in the house with the binoculars—me.

I think he had been waiting knowingly on the verge of this day since last night, when his hoots from up on the knoll spooked our dogs. He knew what was in the wind. And the little birds at the feeder seemed to sense his ominous presence, haunting the field. Raptors stifle the smaller species. As we filtered Sunday's weather reports and watched the pictures from the Midwest storm track, he was no doubt biding his time on some mizzen hackmatack spar. Now he sits thinking—in no rush to leave, settled, solitary, and focused—just like we are, with this surprise pause.

The mice must be thankful for a few inches of snow, with an owl's gaze beating down on their mown metropolis. It is tunnel time, and the deeper the snow the more owl-proof their passages from seed stores to burrows, though I know from past winters that I will eventually see a wing-flutter imprint on the snow just at the surprise terminus of a path of very small footprints. The owl is not here to make snow angels.

The first snow day I remember—when I was in 4th grade—we waited for what seemed an eternity to know if school was cancelled, though it seemed obvious from the power of the storm and the drifts in our driveway. Snow days arrived by radio back then, and our town began with W, putting us at the end of a very long list to be read over the AM news station. "Weston"— finally! Jubilee. Hosannas and praise. Snow angels for sure. And digging. Tunneling.

As soon as the plows had made two passes down our road, my brother and I had all the snow mountains necessary for serious tunneling. The deeper the snow, the greater the challenge. How long a burrow could we engineer without cave-ins? How large an igloo—enough for the whole gang? How many minutes could we endure, on our bellies, in the icy depths? Would Mom ever let us sleep out here in our arctic lair—with flashlights? Would she even find us? Did she know our whereabouts?

Fetch the trowels, buckets, and shovels. On with the snow pants, boots, mittens and hats for a preliminary shift of burrowing, following the fence line along the driveway to the road, then a left turn into the cavern within the *Massif Central* by the mailbox, where we could lie in sodden exhaustion and listen to the beating of our hearts—muffled as mice.

Eventually snow days meant profit. Once we had shoveled our own driveway, lucrative neighborhood jobs awaited. Once, Mrs. Gibson paid me $10.00 when we had twelve inches of snow and her husband was laid up. And to think that our driveway was twice the length of hers. Consider what our conscription saved Dad. But the lure of money wore thin compared with the lure of the gift of a day of leisure, like today, swooping down on us out of the sky, with time drifting up in unexpected corners and the call of neglected books and the authorized complacency in a weekday afternoon nap by the fire.

Yes, a snow day is an owl, descending noiselessly from the treetops on extended woolen wings, inviting us to burrow into memory, silence, and secret mine tunnels.

Something There Is That Does Love a Wall

THEY'RE ALL SNOWED UNDER NOW, like pillows along the roadside for the next four months. But the stone walls hereabout are making a comeback. It's not that they ever went anywhere. They had, however, fallen on hard times through neglect, misunderstanding, and, as it turns out, a dearth of plowing.

I like to think that "something there is that [does] love a wall," to re-paraphrase Robert Frost's musing, walking his boundary wall with his neighbor. On every trip out of town, I see more of these old lichen-encrusted wall stones being realigned on their ancient field-girdling foundations. The ancient wall building rule of "plumb," two over one, one over two to shed water and foil frost, has not been forgotten.

There must be hundreds of miles of stone walls running secretively through the surrounding forests, where only woodcutters and hunters can appreciate them as evidence of things not seen any longer: cleared farmland and old property lines. The most visible walls are the links in a necklace bordering a centuries-old line of sinuous roads running past the old farms of North Castine. Here the Perkins, Wardwell, and Westcott families eked pasture out of forest and farmed for generations. Their small, efficient farmhouses were built snug with the road at a time when five miles per hour was haste. Today I drive the road going ten times that. Modern houses tend to be set back a little farther, at the end of a long driveway.

Arthur Wardwell still owns a huge parcel of pasture down the road from me. The rest of the farms have pretty much given way to new owners, or to descendants of the original families living in small capes or ranch style houses, like the Cyrs. They are summer people, tradesmen, or workers at the paper mill, or excavators, making a living by moving the earth with heavy machinery. Few people are farming anymore, though their farm walls persist—with trees growing through them and toppling the efforts of their forebears. The forest always wants the field back.

Since today's land is not valued for arability, building a new wall has little practical value beyond recreating a certain picturesque quality—the look of New England farmland. Ancient is, of course, relative. It was explained to me recently just why boulders keep migrating to the surface. As trees were felled to make way for farming, frosts penetrated deeper and deeper into the earth. Each winter, freezing and thawing would pry more rocks loose and pinch them upward, like splinters being squeezed to the surface, or wild irises renewing their vigor for spring blooms.

To me, a tightly chinked, straight stone wall, whether newly laid or revived on its old line, is a sign of preservation. New craftsmen are coming along to handle the lapsed stones, and their work is in demand. Mark McCloskey, for instance, has been building a fresh wall, with stones trucked in, at the apple tree verge of the Boninis's fields. And McKie Roth is exhuming the old wall of original fieldstones that fronts his property down the road. You can pull rocks from the earth with a backhoe, but there is no substitute for the knuckle-grating puzzling required to hand-fit stone to stone. It can only be done right in the time-honored, laborious fashion.

I recognize two kinds of commerce going on between the present and the past: craftsmanship and land use. McCloskey is perpetuating a time-honored rural art; Roth is preserving the most enduring vestige of the human impact on forested land. Fieldstone walls mark the time when oxen were used to pull stumps out of nascent fields, and horses followed, tilling the top eight inches for planting grain and hay. Though many fields are kept open even today by annual mowing with a tractor, a lapse of haying for even a single summer would start Arthur Wardwell's large pasture reverting to forest. A wave of sneaky alder is always eyeing open land.

My front walls form part of the Castine necklace, at least the walls out by the road. They have been coming out of dormancy little by little as I clear away the alder trees that have seeped into my front field. A stone wall is not a fence, and alder never misses a chance to jump over and infiltrate. I've been cutting and mowing cedar, fir, birch, and alder from my fields for two years now, reclaiming more room for a large garden, or at least open space.

I like cleared land, and though I'll never restore all my twenty-one acres to the cow pasture they were a hundred years ago, I'm ambitious to have as much garden as the deer will allow me. Just mowing and tilling the small patch I've started on resumes the ritual of bringing spring stones to the walls and adding them to their brethren from an earlier era. "Rocks and alders are the most conspicuous crops," as E.B. White observed. I prefer farming rocks to farming alder.

And the earth is constantly trying to reclaim its rocks. We've gotten an early start on the freezing and thawing that will test and topple stones that are casually stacked. The next winter storms will snap firs and cedars to the forest floor where they'll decay, another annual layer of plant debris, putting the surface at a further and further reach from the rocks below. They are undeterred, however, and I anticipate a bumper rock crop next spring. My walls will surely grow. As to other crops, I hope to get a few rows of corn, beans, and potatoes out of the ground as well. But rocks take far less tending.

The Annual Rings of Christmas

THE FIRST FLAKES OF A NOR'EASTER were already falling as my daughter, Ariel, and I tiptoed across the frozen stream and walked up the hill into our stand of fir trees. She had already scouted a suitable tree to cut, if we could find that tree again for the forest. We had to hurry. The chickadees were hunkering down in the hemlocks. The light was fading, too. But we wanted the right tree, a very tall tree.

The day we get our Christmas tree has always been special. When our kids were younger, I simply brought home the tree from my classroom after the holiday assembly. I just tied it on the roof of my station wagon, strings of popcorn and ragged paper ornaments still attached, ready for its second act in our living room. Our three young kids didn't know that it wasn't a brand-new tree.

A Christmas tree is a miscellany of childhoods, by way of the hand-glued ornaments reminding us of multi-generational school art projects and homespun crafts—some with fingerprints still intact. Out they come: the cookie-cutter stars and reindeer, made of salt dough and embedded sparkles, most of which have decayed into crumbs within a year or two. The miniature Amish quilts, Hilary's second-grade Guatemalan "God's Eyes," and Ariel's ceramic birds endure. School photos pasted on cardboard—Spencer missing his front teeth, me in high school reclining on a motorcycle—are on the tree tonight. Angels and stars rotate into pinnacle service. And lights—lots of little white lights.

Each year we cut a cross-section from the tree trunk, count the rings, and inscribe a note as to who fetched it. We hang the section on the tree the following year, so each year's tree pays tribute to the one preceding. Last year, Hilary, not yet in college, inscribed the ornamental section: "Hilary, Ariel, and Dad cut this down." It dangles now from an upper branch on this year's tree.

My favorite Christmas tree was the year I introduced the model train tradition, when Spencer was four. We started with a large-scale locomotive and a simple circle of track. Each year we've added another boxcar, or more track, until our freight line stretches from the living room into the kitchen—like the old Boston & Maine. I have spent many Christmas hours lying under the tree listening to the realistic clickety-clack, loading and unloading cookies from the flatbed car, sending them over mountain and through tunnels to Spencerville. Train wrecks were Ariel's specialty, parking her baby buggy on the tracks to impress and infuriate her brother at the controls.

Ariel and I found the pre-selected tree before dark but noticed a disqualifying bald side to it. We trudged further up the hill and inspected a few more possibilities. Too tall, too thin, too sparse. Finally: just right. I sawed through the frozen trunk and Ariel tipped it gently to the ground. We grabbed the lower branches and dragged it base-first toward the house, as the dogs nipped playfully at the top.

During the two years we lived in California, we New Englanders were a bit disoriented when it came time to find a

Christmas tree. The kids were still wearing shorts. There was no letup to the perfect summer weather. And nowhere to go to cut a fresh tree. We mail-ordered one from L.L. Bean, I'm ashamed to say. A Maine spruce arrived on our doorstep in a cardboard box, after undergoing a mandatory quarantine. A state agriculture agent inspected it before we could bring it inside. Out came the box of ornaments. Up went the angels, globes, glued Popsicle sticks, five-year-old candy canes, and photos. And the train. In a desert climate you can assemble the tracks out in the driveway. We ran our now trans-continental freight service (renamed the Union Pacific that year) right through the garden.

Tonight, Ariel and I manage to wrestle the tree through the front door and into its heavy cast-iron stand. It turns the house inside out, radiating the deep cold of the woods and perfuming the living room with its sap. The tip brushes the ceiling—a new height record. Now it is ornament time. We spiral 600 little white lights down the tree, from tip to floor. Bangor and Aroostook freight service will resume shortly. Ornaments may wear out, but Spencerville always awaits cookies. We will always deliver.

A Line in Winter

A CLOTHESLINE IN WINTER—how forlorn!

Mine is like a wire missing its birds, a musical measure bereft of notes, or a branch bare of leaves. A winter clothesline is silence. Blankness. Waiting. Unfulfilled expectation. Lost purpose. Dormancy. Torpor. Something's not there among the clothespins left languishing on the line, and it reminds us of exactly what it is that's not there.

In winter, for a while, the clothesline is my thermometer; a laundry barometer. It's the freezing line below which nothing will hang to dry, at least until the sun peers around the roof ridge line, gladdening the dooryard tundra. You don't need a weatherman to know which way the wind blows—a clothesline will do.

One man's freezing point is another man's dried jeans and underwear, lest your twisted knickers come off the clothesline like so many rough-sawn boards. Might as well stack them like cordwood where the sun permeates the el. The clothesline is an air-dried-clothes dowsing rod: it will find evaporation if it is there to be found.

Our line regales us with the invisible dance between freezing and thawing, drying and persistent damp. On a windy day, the socks and trousers dance. And how do you tell these dancers from their dance? Watch. Surely in mid-winter we reach a clothesline equinox, the boundary between indoor and outdoor laundry drying, when a brief thaw will inspire an ecstatic bloom of myriad garments in the local dooryards. A line in winter beckons in a thaw.

Alas, it used to be the sole way to dry. Now, it is the outlier. Bring back the clothesline! It is more than the sum of its simple parts. A clothesline flies the flags of order and intention. It exhibits the homeowner's strategy. Shirts and pants hung to dry practically fold and crease themselves. Surely Thoreau would appreciate the economy in that, like the firewood maxim attributed to him: My logs warmed me twice, "once while I was splitting them, and again when they were on the fire."

My wife loves a full clothesline. "It says, 'Someone's home.'" It flies the standard of the homeowner, indicating residence, like a baronial pennant.

She's not alone. "I counted eight, one for each day of the week," said another clothesline aficionado, appreciating her neighbor's plaid shirts. "One security shirt and one for current wear. He's a true engineer." Transcendentalism inhabits the adjacent backyards.

The clothesline has a graphic allure. Our favorite paintings in any medium are clotheslines. Perhaps even in their static, two-dimensional state, they inevitably suggest motion, wind power, and the alchemy of evaporation. And they have that horizon line that draws our vision far into the side yard frame, just like a New England seascape.

A walk around town would aid the discussion, except fewer and fewer clotheslines persist. Doesn't everyone know that good clotheslines make good neighbors? I won't comment on your tighty whiteys; you lay off my bleach accidents and crimson union suits. We're lettin' it all hang out. Our unmentionables are airing out properly, luxuriating for a few hours in the sun.

And there is nothing like clean sheets, spinnakering in the breeze for an afternoon before battening down the mattress for a fragrant nap. Clotheslines are backyard schooners, four sheets to the wind.

Engineer mind: Surely there is an equation for the air-dry, latent energy conservation coefficient of the clothesline at work (or is it at rest?) on a summer day in coastal Maine? Inquiring Yankee minds want to know the carbon offsets for a week's worth of flannel shirts, attached with regulation clothespins, arms hanging below, shirttails above, one sunny morning in Maine. What is the drying time, divided by number of shirts, length of line, temperature and relative humidity, versus an equivalent bundle of shirts in an electric or gas dryer? Factor in on-shore or off-shore breezes. And wind speed. Fabric must also be a consideration. Cotton, wool, polyester; a blend? Surely this too affects drying.

The conclusion is clear: line dry your garments and linen. The carbon offsets are inestimable, as are the aesthetic benefits.

And what about the emotional offsets—the ecstatic response to the fragrance, say, of a sundried flannel shirt? Sheets perfumed by adjacent lilacs? The loft of cotton pillowcases lovingly tussled dry near a spruce grove, *sans* drier sheets—back when clotheslines last in the dooryard bloom'd?

Adieu—for now, we are forlorn.

The Cape Racer
and Other
Heirloom Sounds

I MISS THE CAPE RACER. Even though I have yet to ride on one, its poetry of design and acoustic sculpting make it audible to my imagination. According to legend, Martin Van Buren Gray, of Deer Isle, invented it in 1882. It was a wooden sled with metal runners and a flexible, ladder-like frame that was used to haul smelt-fishing supplies—and, presumably, fish—on and off Maine's frozen lakes. And it was used to race down Perkins Hill, or from the four corners, or along the South Penobscot Road by the Chocolate Church, in an era that had much less traffic.

I thought of it when I heard some of our senior citizens talking about flying along the backroads on their Cape Racers, with sentinels strategically placed to forestall collisions with cars and trucks. The only way to stop was to roll off. And I envy their other recollections of riding to school on snowy days "on the back of my father's snowshoes," as some of them used to do.

All is not lost. My neighbor, David "Cappy" Wardwell, an eighth-generation Mainer, makes them. Neat rows of various unique models line his shed. He uses yellow birch, the traditional oak, or ash for the slender frames, and metal runners canted at an angle, putting the inside edge on the ice or snow to carve a sure, straight track. Each one is signed and numbered, lovingly crafted in the winter when weather drives work inside— beautifully sanded and varnished, each a sculpture in its own right, and the embodiment of engineering finesse and speed, form and terrifyingly fast function. There are no brakes. To bail on your trajectory, roll off.

Losing old objects and practices made me think of a hidden extinction. I wondered about the lost sounds familiar in former times. How many people remember the *sound* of such a sled carving an icy road, or the creaking sound of an old leather snowshoe harness? What else are we missing from our sonic environment—or in danger of losing?

One of the earliest sounds I can remember was the rotary blade, hand-propelled lawnmower. It is a mnemonic of time and place, and I miss it, in part, because it opens the rich possibilities of recollections released by savoring sound. We are accustomed to seeing old photos. Old sounds are more or less confined to music or film. We should start a new concept: the mind's ear.

Mr. Hankner, our next-door neighbor during my toddler-to-third-grade years, mowed his immaculate lawn on summer evenings just beneath my bedroom window and I loved to hear the rattling, clipping-clatter, winding noise of his ancient, sharp, well-oiled hand mower.

Reaching the end of each row, he would turn to come back to the top of the yard, the blades whirring freely as he realigned himself for the return trip. His yard was a postage stamp of grass, but he kept it trimmed with regimental precision. After mowing, he would put the nozzle on his hose and water the lawn, and

I would drift off to sleep lulled by the soft hissing of artificial rain on his roses, peonies, and velvet grass.

Whenever I tried to use our own hand mower, it never made the pleasing sewing-machine sounds of Mr. Hankner's—just huffing and puffing. My own huffing and puffing. I begged Dad for a gas-powered mower, and efficiency eventually won over aural tradition.

Dad liked calligraphy pens. I loved the scratching sound that he made as he practiced Cyrillic letters—even his signature had a Cyrillic look to it. Imagine the sound of ice skates scoring a pond and you have the sound of his pen on paper. Needless to say, the sound of dipping pen in ink is also an extinct whisper now.

Words make a kind of heirloom sound too. Many are linked with a type of landscape that is fast disappearing, or inhabitants of the landscape who are no longer around to describe it—like snowshoe tail riders. We have a lot of great words for flowing water—rapids, rips, riffles and rills, seeps and sinks—that aren't in frequent use. Certainly, those water sounds and distinctive ways of running downhill haven't gone away. But would it be fair to say there are fewer people who will stop and listen to it, and use the tried and true names for the particular qualities of such flow?

I just learned the term "jackstraw timber," apt descriptor for the jumbled thickets created when a stand of trees has enough fallen or blown-down members to resemble the old children's game called pick-up sticks—an heirloom game . . . remember the sound of the sticks falling?

We are, of course, making new heirloom sounds all the time. Some of today's most common sounds may be destined for the sound heap of history, like Mr. Hankner's mower. Perhaps the internal combustion engine is a future heirloom sound. One can only hope so. It would help restore the sound of riffles of water.

Even if the old sounds are gone, it's never too late to restore an appreciation of the subtleties of experience hidden in simple sonic places. Has anyone heard the sound of one hand clapping recently? I think a full woodshed has a sound—full volume. So does an empty space—not echoing, but the simple sound of volume unfilled. Listen, if you can. Silence is an heirloom sound too. John Keats heard it: "And then there crept a little noiseless noise among the leaves, Born of the very sigh that silence heaves."

I hope that kind of non-sound will always be savored in living memory.

The Two-Tongued Sea

THE ASSIGNMENT FOR THE 7TH and 8th graders was to select one of Dylan Thomas's topic sentences, each borrowed from a paragraph of "A Child's Christmas in Wales," and use it to begin their own recollection of their local or familial holidays. We had read Thomas's wonderful story, watched an excellent film version of it, and looked outside as the snow hushed Castine—inspiring writing weather, to be sure, for kids in a harbor town in a Northern latitude.

You could begin, "One Christmas was so much like another, in those years. . . ." Or perhaps you preferred, "All the Christmases roll down toward the two-tongued sea. . . ." I am fond of this one: "There are always Uncles at Christmas." With such prompts, it was important to review two crucial writing rules: Never let the facts get in the way of a good story. And, it's all true, even if it never happened. It was time to stretch out and inhabit the feeling of the season in words, to don the mantel of Thomas and Wales and merge wolves in Wales with Castine, with cherished candy, mittens, firemen, and tipsy aunts.

"Bring out the tall tales now that we told by the fire," wrote Thomas.

And so we plunged our hands in and brought out the memory of the year Olivia and J.C. made the snow dog, instead of snowman, and named him Veggie Bob Dog, due to his broccoli eyes, cauliflower nose, and carrot mouth. On the same day, they invented jelly snowballs. "You have to pack the snow together, and dig a little hole in it," said J.C.—which tasted disgusting, according to Olivia.

Christmas means movies: *Willy Wonka and the Chocolate Factory*, *White Christmas, The Nutcracker*, or the ubiquitous Grinch. Surely, he is one of the salty, bitter tongues of the sea of Christmas: the spoiler, the gift thief, and the humbug.

What about the uncles, or aunts, or visiting cousins—nonnies and nannies and oomas? One uncle lived in a tepee, with the ornaments and decorations hung from the poles inside. Christmas in California has a way of becoming a cultural adventure for travelers from the East.

Any forest dweller knows that choosing exactly the right tree is "a very annoying yet rewarding job." With hundreds to choose from, it's hard to detect "the perfect one for you, your family, and of course, your house." Alex defined the rubric for choice: not "too tall or too short, too narrow or too wide, too wet or too dry, too brown or too green, too small or too big, too many branches or too few, too saggy or too lopsided."

And once the tree is correctly placed, bringing the outside in, and turning the house inside out with the aroma of spruce or fir, the decorating begins. "I get the white, wooden snowflake," writes Meredith, "and Sawyer gets the wooden moose that has a string attached to make its leg move when you pull it. We hang them on a different branch and go back to get the next ornaments. We hang up angels with newspaper for wings, Pillsbury dough men, cupcakes with shiny pink and green frosting and Minnie and Mickey Mouse Bobbleheads. Then, we grab our mugs and Dad puts another log in the fire and we sit back to play a few card games and enjoy our work."

Who wants a useful present, "such as warm, fluffy hats and soft, handmade scarves, socks and white T-shirts?" You can't play with T-shirts, thought Gabriel. Uncle Ely to the rescue: "There appeared a blue Yamaha RC snowmobile, with batteries." Think of all the mystery, majesty, and quasi-ecclesiastical authority in the phrase, "There appeared." Game Boys we have heard on high, sweetly beeping all o'er Maine.

What would Dylan Thomas say? "Years and years ago, when I was a boy, when there were remote-controlled, battery-operated Big Wheels in Wales. . . ." It's hard to hear the absence of the sound of snow filling the fir boughs above the mechanical whine and torque of the latest radio toy vehicle.

There are essential letters. "I was worried whether I had been clear enough in my letter to Santa," wrote Madison. "I had asked for a Barbie car. There was a lot at stake this Christmas, and it was my first letter to Santa. I was four."

There are snow days, gifts of leisure time packaged and delivered with the actual raw materials of fantastic winter play. Not too many snow days, please, lest we find ourselves paying for them with school days in July—a high interest rate, to be sure—just enough. "The huge snowdrifts from the plow make excellent forts," wrote Meredith, "and the pile of snow at the bottom of the slide is soft and powdery from the dry wind and freezing air." After a full day of such cold-pile jumping, "a hot cocoa with extra marshmallows and a peppermint stick" waits inside.

And finally, we all close our eyes with something like this favorite Christmas poem by Bill Watterson: "Tomorrow's what I'm waiting for, but I can wait a little more." We can all feel what it's like to think, just before slumber, as Thomas did, "I could see the lights in the windows of all the other houses on our hill and hear the music rising from them up the long, steady falling night. I turned the gas down, I got into bed. I said some words to the close and holy darkness, and then I slept." And we can all hear the other tongue of the sea, lapping at the silken shore of memory and care: And there appeared, Peace.

Blinter

One good word is worth a thousand pictures.

—Eric Sevareid

IN THE BEGINNING WAS THE WORD for the crisp, clarion, cold sharp light that only comes in winter. And the word was with winter. And the word was *blinter*. The best way to define blinter is simply to experience the light of January or February, from star or sun.

And because this is a Northern Scots word, I like to think I am channeling the ancestral ken of an ancient grandfather Neilson (for that's probably what we were, being Norse incomers to Scotland) standing on the headlands in Caithness and looking east. "Och, 'tis a right blintery day," he would have said, I imagine, as he squinted toward the sea that brought him or his forebears to Scotland. It works just as well for me looking Bagaduce River-ward across our field in late afternoon winter sun, or upward into the blintery cosmos. Orion is surely a blinter constellation, for instance. It sure feels close.

We can also look down at our feet, appreciating the crystalline blinter of the field of powdery snow in full sun, forcing us to squint at the tracks left by night visitors . . . owl-wing impressions astride ominous talon-prints. There is too much light, too much sparkle—an intensity unrivaled by any other seasonal lumens. It can be accompanied by *aingealach*, or "acute numbness in great frost." Or you might enjoy the use of the word *apracity:* "the warmth of the sun in winter," a word that seems to have come in and out of usage around 1623. Do we need it back?

We don't make words like we used to. Language and experience used to be more intertwined. Words held a far more tactile value; onomatopoeia was rampant. We didn't Google for the lexicon of snow descriptors, but, like the Eskimos, imagined how a word might embody its very meaning. Blinter does so. It hits our ear like a musical, rather than an etymological, note—an actual sound that blends feeling with descriptive force. The best words have sensory roots.

Inherited words are waning and our vocabulary shrinking. Extremes of temperature and precipitation require new language when the customary words just don't do justice to what our senses are experiencing. But contemporary word creation seems to come increasingly from small, smug gestures or opinionated intellectual connections—as "blog" is to "conversation." New words are punchlines, tag lines, etymological schemes. They are small, trite—sitcom scale, not epic.

I like Philip Booth's phrase for the blinter experience in his poem "A Man in Maine." An old man's final words, exhaled as he chopped wood outside the back door, and recalled by his son:

> *this time of*
> *year the stars*
> *come close some fierce.*

Enough said. Imagine your own eyes taking in that starlight. See what I mean? One good word brings immediacy and power without working too hard at intellectual precision—brings the stars fearsomely closer. Have you needed this word this winter? You knew exactly what it felt like at first sight. Soon, you'll need *faoilleachd,* the Gaelic word for "the last three weeks of winter and the first three weeks of spring." It's what we in Maine just call March hill.

Plowing by Woods on a Winter Evening

A NOR'EASTER HAS US in its talons—finally.

The entire East Coast has been hammered, there is a record twenty-two inches of snow in New York's Central Park, and this storm might just bury us too.

It has taken until mid-February for a proper winter storm to arrive here in Castine. The kids in town feel cheated with only one snow day from school, and the playground has been devoid of snow for forts and sliding. It just hasn't been an authentic Maine winter.

"We don't have storms like we used to," says Denny Colson, thirty-year veteran of the town's public works crew. He is one of the three men charged with keeping eighteen miles of roads passable tonight. "I've seen snow up over the store windows downtown," he adds. A good storm brings out the plowman's blizzard nostalgia.

"We had to cut through trees with a chainsaw to get down Madockawando and La Tour streets," says Denny, recalling the ice storm of '98. "The crew worked sixty hours straight."

Castine, a tidy little four-hundred-year-old town at the end of a peninsula in Penobscot Bay, is the kind of proverbial Maine village where no one locks their doors or takes the keys out of the car ignition.

Downtown hasn't changed much since a hundred years ago, when the budget for "snow removal" was $200, mostly to pay laborers who came behind the blizzard and shoveled. One of those men on the payroll in 1906 was Pearl Colson, Denny's great-grandfather. He earned $2.27 for the season. Then came the Model T truck with a plow, changing snow removal.

Back then the whole town budget amounted to about $14,000. Today's budgets are numbers with two commas. This year, the line for winter sand and salt alone is $40,000, plus $20,000 for equipment maintenance, and $120,000 in crew salaries.

No one likes to drive the snowplow down Green Street, the trickiest street in town because of a steep incline that ends abruptly on Water Street. If you don't make this right-hand turn, there's nowhere to go but over the embankment and into Eaton's boatyard. The cable barrier could restrain a car. The plow truck, however, will likely take the barrier with it on its way over the embankment and into Kenny Eaton's second floor office.

Denny knows. He put the plow truck over the guardrail once. It scared Jute Mixer, his wingman at the time, enough that he bailed out, jumping from the truck right over the wing plow. The truck ended up teetering over the embankment. Denny thought it safer to stay with the vehicle.

Stories of plowing calamities abound. No driver is spared. Like the time Denny couldn't see the road and turned into Guild's field. "Geezum, Jute," Denny said, "this road's getting awful rough." He kept going, plowing up the field, and eventually found his way back to the main road.

Or the "time we hit a car over by the post office," says Denny. "Larry, or one of us, dropped the wing on it."

Today the snow is blowing sideways, drifting along the village lanes. At least sixteen hours of plowing lie ahead for the three men who share the duty. Henry Erhard has drawn the first eight-hour shift and will take me along for a ride.

Henry is a Coast Guard veteran whose family has lived in Castine for seven generations. As we bounce along, he eyes the plow's marker wands, using six control levers beside his seat to adjust the pitch and yaw of the blade. With the sanding control box on the floor, he adjusts the volume and pattern of the sand spraying off the hopper at the back of the truck, amidst constant gear-shifting. The effect is muffled thunder as we push snow to the side of deserted streets.

You always want to be making right turns," Henry says, as he heads the blue Chevy down Battle Avenue toward the light-house. Clearly, he is working hard to anticipate the potholes, frost heaves, curbs, and manhole covers. There are telephone poles and trees for that wing blade to catch on, as well as parked cars, pedestrians, and street signs. Henry points out myriad deep plow gouges on poles.

We drive a series of concentric circles beginning at the west end of town. From the lighthouse we turn down Perkins Street, pass Fort Madison, then follow Tarratine Street to Main Street, then down the hill past the post office, bank, and Big Ernie's Variety. Then Henry does the route in reverse to clear the other side of the streets.

"The woods are lovely, dark and deep," but the truck is getting lighter and we have miles to go before refilling the sand hopper out at the town dump.

"Truck weight? I don't know," says Henry. "I can tell how much sand is left by how it drives." Weight is crucial: traction is only as good as the amount of sand on board. In seven years of plow driving, he has gone off the road only once. His truck was too light going up Windmill Hill, but Denny managed to back it out of the ditch. A rookie mistake. Henry has not, however, plowed Guild's field with the truck.

Here comes Green Street.

"It doesn't look too bad today," says Henry, downshifting urgently. "If it gets too slick, I can always lower the wing blade and hook it on that fire hydrant and pivot around the corner." That's the last chance gambit to keep the truck out of Eaton's office. As Denny says, "it's not in the manual, but it works." I'm prepared to bail.

The truck lurches, groans and inches right around the corner and safely onto Water Street. Phew. Time for lap two of the town. Two hours down, another six to go.

As he drops me off, Henry takes a lug wrench to his front left wheel and cranks down hard on the bolts. He had detected a wobble. The ten-year-old truck is due for replacement—a $65,000 item that is not in this year's budget.

Snug at home, Larry Redman must be watching Storm Center updates on television, and Denny has probably gone to bed early to be ready for the last shift, the one that will prepare the roads for Monday morning. Meanwhile, many a Castine kid is hoping that the plow will not keep ahead of the snowfall, and they'll have a day off from school.

Denny, however, may not even need to plow. The snow stops at midnight. We don't have storms like we used to. "If we had the snow we had back then," says Denny, "people wouldn't know what to do with it." Blizzard nostalgia.

As it turns out, school starts as usual on Monday. And even in New York, schools open the day after their old-time, Castine-size snowstorm. They got *our* snow.

Winter Nears Its Tipping Point

AT A CERTAIN POINT, late in February, there comes a day when you realize that you are pivoting.

The junipers may still be shagged with ice and fishing shacks still colonizing the lakes. No one yet dares to remove the snow tires. However, you can feel a gentle shift of weight. It's like the heavy keel of a sailboat, unseen below the waterline, counterbalancing a tack to port; like the moment you crest a hill and go from climbing to descending; like the switch from peddling hard against inertia to coasting with gravity.

Something Gene said to me further defined the pivotal moment: "A day like this gives you hope." As he bagged my milk and potato chips at the checkout counter, Gene was inspired by the sunny, warm, late winter vibe of this Sunday in Maine. Around here we skip "paper or plastic?" and cut to the existential chase.

"Newton's laws make it fairly predictable," I replied. I know only a smidgeon about the laws of Sir Isaac's physics, save a vague sense of their description of bodies in motion staying reliably in motion—a universal constant that orders local changes, the scientific explanation for today's climatic poetry.

The aforementioned climb starts when folks here on the coast hunker down for winter. We draw in, close up, and pull boats out of the water—literally and figuratively. I've noticed a tendency to hunch over a little bit, heading into the teeth of December's cold and dark, then truly button up for January's storms. Then, when a February day such as this arrives, it is a welcome augury. You can relax just a little, shrug, then rebound and rise up like birches after an ice storm. We lighten—there are twenty more minutes of daylight this week, we realize. The celestial bodies are truly in motion. Orion's days are numbered. The summer constellations await, just over the southern horizon, yearning to return. Winter must relax its talons after all, dropping us to the meadow. We will find ourselves among lambs in clover, gamboling down the long meadow to summer.

First, however, there are stages like thermoclines to pass through, beginning with fuel. As I look down the slope toward March, this climbing down is embedded with an expectation of "making it." When Gary's Fuel pulls up in his blue truck to fill our oil tank, it will take fewer gallons than last week. The furnace rumbles less frequently, for shorter, almost token bursts, since the sun is higher, toasting the front rooms farther into the afternoon to the delight of the cats luxuriating on the windowsills. Our cellar firewood pile shrinks but looks like it will be enough for the next few weeks of woodstove fires. In early February, I worried about there being not enough. Now, I know we will make it to the day when we need no longer augment the passive solar heat.

The next phase is mud. Just two days ago we could rely on frozen ground everywhere—no fear of getting sucked into the soft shoulder of the road. Now everywhere it will be mud, the shallower frost a message to woodcutters in particular, that they have only a little time to finish skidding trees for next year's cordwood before the ground will no longer support their tires. The final push is on! Whereas yesterday our car and truck had been immobilized on ice; today they are immobilized in dark oozing paste. It will freeze over nightly, elasticize by mid-morning, and then record critter traffic: four cats, one large dog, sundry squirrels, raccoons, porcupine, and deer foraging amongst the neighbor's cedars.

Coming soon: skunks. My thoughts shift to other arrivals: friends reporting sightings of birds they have not seen or heard in months. The very notion of things returning is itself a key harbinger. The appearance of an early cardinal is a vibrant proof of Newton's second law.

Next: seeds. Talk among gardeners turns to seed catalogs long before the soil can be forked. I was thinking "seeds" when I discovered four storm windows languishing by a dumpster, just right to cover the cold frames we're building, I unscrewed them from their gaunt, discarded window frames and trucked them home. Potting soil packs on windowsills will sprout and cold weather crops will begin to harden a few hours at a time in the frames. Of course, peas go right into the ground on St. Patrick's Day, defiant of any forecast, even snow. Newton's second law predicts an August zucchini glut.

Finally: buds. If we're yearning, it won't be long until a few lilac sprigs from the side yard can be clipped and vased indoors, forced to corroborate the inevitable: spring is truly just ahead, with blooms. The resident poet best defines my sense of this climb down from winter:

> *Now March, in noon sun,*
> *a small snowfield, bright*
> *as a high arctic summer.*
> *Deep in glanced light,*
> *old stonewalls tumble*

through conifers, back
in woodlots without
a leaf left, far from
October's gold leaves
hat blind a man, or tug
him toward May's first
green to replay Eden.[1]

We are so *there.*

---

1. "Reach Road: In Medias Res," Philip Booth.

Spring

The Force That Through the Green Fuse Drives the Flower Drives Us

THE FLOWER'S FUSE HAS BEEN LIT, and so have our spring yearnings. The equinox may operate like clockwork, thanks to celestial mechanics—the image of gears and springs and levers is appropriate for the automaticity of the forthcoming season—but the bursting of that flower from the bud is more spontaneous and loosely improvised, depending on local conditions of rain, clouds, temperature and sunshine. Celestial mechanics may drive the big picture, but at ground level it may come down to on- or off-shore breezes, the time by which fog burns off, the elevation of hill and dale—micro-climate factors. And there's always a warm side to a building where daffodils cozy along the foundation and plot to ambush the unexpecting.

Who knew that the younger, smaller trees debut before the older, taller trees, that the weather down on the forest floor, like ocean thermoclines, is not the same as that up in the canopy, where winter's temps persist. It's warmer at ground level. It's still cold on high. There raptor winter still has a perch, its talons out for a downward swoop, talons out.

Trees know what time it is. They also know what time it *feels* like. "In the spring, the young trees . . . leaf out two weeks before the large trees, ensuring themselves a long leisurely breakfast in the sun," explains Peter Wohlleben. Breakfast is where the syrup is. And that's where we too are expectantly seated—around the "table" on the forest floor, soaking in any available light and heat, gauging whether this might be the day to cast off winter coats, roll up our flannel sleeves and bud, leaf out, go for it. Sure, there may be another snow, but it can only be a fleeting ground cover, right? Even a sodden, plowable driveway covering couldn't persist for long. Tick tock. Open-water fishing is ahead. We are in spring training.

And doesn't spring make us *feel* like those saplings? Perhaps we are a little hunched over by ice and snow, branches broken, bark torn by a deer, a little timid, untrusting of the persistence of cold, wary of shocking our new growth at the tips of our branches, while starting the next annual ring deep in our heartwood. But, by god, we're encouraged by the elasticity of mud, and we too will have sap flowing to our feet—shoots and leaves doing their vernal best to warm up and force themselves to appear, our tuberous souls stirring.

There are but three months until lupines flower, four until raspberries ripen. Bears, too, are stirring in contemplative fitful slumber, appetites recharging, dreaming of low-hanging bird feeders. Can a premature robin be too far distant? Somewhere the early bird is watching the changing constellations and thinking, "The worm, the worm!" Or are we too that bird? The force that to the bird feeder brunch drives the black bear drives us.

March Hill

THE WILD THINGS ARE ON THE MOVE. Yesterday, while the full moon leered through the fir trees, I passed two skunks meandering on the verge of the road at dusk. At the Unitarian Church in town, Larry Redman has set out the traps to try and relocate the amorous skunk pairs from beneath the parish hall—again. He gets $30 per skunk. One whiff suggests they are reluctant to be moved. Larry will need better bait.

At 4:00 a.m. today, my dogs raise a ruckus. Out on the front yard a fox is dancing beneath the sunflower seed feeder, digging for kernals. Or is he digging into the mice tunnels fanning out from the feeder drop zone? Is he desperately hungry, or jubilant at such easy pickings?

Friday was a snow day from school, and as I trudged through the heavy wet snowfall out to the mailbox at midday, and paused in the cold, I heard a most unexpected, unmistakable sound. From somewhere in the treetops a robin was singing. Hungry, or jubilant? I listened intently for a few minutes. Sure enough, here on the second day of March, and the third snow day from school, with the winter storm warning not due to expire for another few hours, a harbinger of spring had appeared. Later in the day, two more robins appeared at the feeder. Got worms? Too soon. Not for a while.

These deceptive contrasts and tensions are what make March a "hill"—a unique season, here in Maine. We're counting *down* to spring, but trudging *up* through snow, then mud, frost heaving roads, and sunnier but blustery days. Then, perhaps, it could even snow again, or the dread "wintery mix" that the meteorologists use to hedge their forecasts and blur the snow-rain line. Then the sap starts to flow and the cold nights and warm days express sugar from trees—what alchemy. If we can make it to Maple Sunday at the end of the month, the nouveau syrup vintage will be ready. Days of freezing and thawing will have done their job. And hidden beneath the snow cover, "The force that through the green fuse drives the flower," as Dylan Thomas wrote, *is* driving the flower. Can forsythia be far behind?

March gnaws at us. And the March forest slowly relinquishes its grip on certain macabre winter artifacts. My dog, Gus, drags a deer leg from the cedar grove—a trophy melted out of a drift like the Neolithic hunter surfacing from the alpine glacier. Gus is loathe to surrender the tasty limb. He growls. He means it. I back off. March is like that too.

We begin to feel spring's struggle to arrive—or is that feeling really just the flexing of our own wild yearnings, still held in the traces of winter? We have an overriding sense of being *between.* We remain in the grip of Old Man Winter, even as a crazy, misguided robin catches an early flight home from somewhere southern and warm . . . where Orion is now heading for the summer—our summer, that is.

I brace stoically for March. On the other hand, I feel that my looking ahead, when it's grounded in aspiration, pulls me forward. There's a lot to do in March that makes us feel eager, and spreads creative energy and even momentum. March is full of new things to aspire to, rather than muddle through. The robins know.

The school year has a way of layering and overlapping these cycles. At my school, we have a daily morning meeting. We do a daily count to mark our progress. It might go as follows: today is the 110th day of school and the 75th day of winter. There are 15 days until the spring equinox, 65 more school days this year. Thanks to the snow day, the last day of school will now be June 18th—three days before the summer solstice, the longest day of the year. Yes, March is a countdown and a hill.

This ragged month *will* be over, though today it seems so stubbornly persistent. And then we'll begin the next countdown—the 79 days until the start of the next school year in September. Once again, we'll be living between school seasons, while savoring the height of the celestial one we'll be in at the time. The new wild things will be on the move: baby skunks under the church and fox kits in my field. We too will be on the move, fulfilling warm summer aspirations and yearnings stirred in March. They tend to eclipse the muddy path it's taken to arrive. On March hill we earn our July meadow, before trudging back to cold again.

Learning the Lore of My Land

THE RUCKUS OUTSIDE was just the dogs giving their welcome bark to Mr. Cyr, my neighbor who inhabits the white farmhouse to our south. He was standing in my dooryard, on this day of frozen ground on the cusp of spring, waiting to see who might be home.

"I've just come from your corner property marker," he said. "I thought you might like to see exactly where it is."

He had traipsed through the muddy woods to make his first visit to our land since we'd purchased it. I went for my boots, eager to walk our common property line with the man who knew more about my woods than I. It was the perfect day for it: cool, but not cold; bright, but not sunny; the air moving softly through branches preparing for buds, the sap surely flowing. A week before and the snow would have been too high; now the snow was gone, but the frost had not yet lifted and the bugs were not out—just right for an afternoon walk.

When we met up in town a few weeks before, Mr. Cyr had started to acquaint me with the historical contours of this land. I was full of questions about our 21 acres, its ownership and care prior to our time on it. The land itself tells some of the obvious story—vestigial orchards, stone walls, rusty fencing, a rusted bucket, and ancient wagon traces, to say nothing of deer antlers, owl pellets, bird nests, and various burrows left by its critter denizens.

The approximate average tree age gives a rough timeline for some of its prior use—the fact that some acres were plowed, some used as pasture, some as orchard—and the approximate time at which an owner stopped clearing the always encroaching forest. The forest wants the cleared land back. Trees want to resume forestation and have waited patiently for a chance during these few hundred years of human effort at keeping the land cleared for farming. Stand by any stone wall and you're standing in a former field, regardless of the current thicket of fir, cedar, birch, or pine that has moved back in. These rocks nicked someone's plow and were then dropped on the boundary line to stay out of the way once and for all.

My oldest trees are seventy years old, except for a few ancient white pines up on the knoll, something Mr. Cyr confirmed from living memory.

"My wife Lois's father stopped clearing these pastures in about 1930," he said, as we walked along our common property line. It was Moore Farm then. I could make out an old farm lane and wire fencing and posts collapsing into the ground. He is all cedar and I am all alder now, at this spot where a pasture used to be and is now thick with seventy-year-old trees.

I imagine my field with Mr. Cyr's father-in-law's cows on it, turning through the gate and heading home to the milking barn. I have already cleared out the young alder and have spent the winter taking down bigger trees to enlarge the clearing. We want more open land for gardening; but it also feels as if we are resuming where an old farmer left off.

In the past 300 years, this Maine peninsula in general has never been as forested as it is now. Cleared land was valuable, more useful and productive. And no one wanted property on the shore! How things change. Now everyone wants a water view. I prefer to look at trees.

"Lois's father put in this fence," said Mr. Cyr. "Unrolled it from a cart drawn by oxen." Lois had grown up on this land and remembered when there was a cornfield in the big level area on the other side of our knoll. It's alder and cedar now, with a few wild apple trees, but that explains the old milk cans rusting into the ground at the bottom of the hill, where the stream outlet runs.

"Beavers dammed this up and that ruined the corn field," said Mr. Cyr. We tiptoed over a log to cross the stream and trudged up a small hill covered with birch and fir trees, and then along another stone wall I had never seen before. Behold the iron stake and orange blaze: our back corner.

"I never thought to look for my back line over this way," I told Mr. Cyr. "I was looking in the wrong place." My bearings were off, and I discovered that we owned more land than I had known.

Or rather, knowing your 21 acres on paper is quite different from walking a physical boundary line with your neighbor. Neat lines on a survey map give a sense of volume and shape; walking over muddy, frozen cedar roots and jumping an icy stream restore its full and proper texture and dimension. There are birch trees and white pines that became mine that day, and clearings on a hillside overlooking the old corn field that will make a pleasant spot for a summer picnic.

And there is lore. Through Mr. Cyr, I can envision the farmer whose cows used to graze the woods that I will soon call pasture once again.

Mr. Cyr and I parted, and he returned to his woodlot while I walked back to our house down the old farm road in the center of our lot.

As I walked over the knoll, I wondered about the story of our northern boundary, where another stone wall, with a rusted bucket poking through, runs from the Castine Road back to the alder thicket that I will now call by its ancient name: the corn field.

The Vizier of Native Brook Trout

ED IS THE VIZIER OF BROOK TROUT in our town. And now that the water level is high with the spring run-off, the beaver dam flowage swollen, the brooks running in spate as the ice in the lakes dissipates, the water temperature inching upward with every sunny day, it is time for me to ask Ed if he will reveal another of his secret fishing holes. Please.

I am beguiled by the stories of myth and legend: of Ed herding 14-inch brook trout right over beaver dams and into his creel with only a few articulate whistles; calling trout by name to move them from pool to pool, lest they fall into undeserving hands; guiding Those Deemed Worthy to his secret spots blindfolded, by night, in the interest of sanctity and preservation. I could go on. I am told he has photos encapsulating some extraordinary days of fishing on the local streams. But which streams—that will always be the question.

Am I worthy? He guards them assiduously, cautious about divulging too much of an activity that has taken on the aspect of a life's work, of conservation verging on guardianship. After many months of discussion and prompting, Ed gave me actual directions, not allusions, to a fishing spot. Not, alas, with the aid of a map. This was a challenge. His reference points are vague, or colloquial. Directions such as "turn left where Andy Snow used to live, then go along 'til you see that big spruce that was struck by lightning last summer . . . the fishing hole is in the brook just below there" do not always do the trick. Perhaps Ed is aware of that.

He talks with much more exacting fervor and detail about his own excursions and tantalizing successes. "I could have caught my limit last Sunday," he has told me. Or, "By Golly, weren't they just jumping onto the hook yesterday," he has told me. "I caught the biggest brook trout that you ever laid eyes on just standing on the beaver dam down by . . . " he has told me, before lapsing into directions to the dam too cryptic to be the least bit useful. Perhaps Ed is aware of that.

I suppose I am his "sport," in the old Maine guide usage: the sportsman from "away" who needs help stalking wild quarry. Before making Ed's acquaintance, I would spend hours driving to fishing spots due to the received wisdom that one had to go to the next county inland from the coast of Penobscot Bay before finding worthwhile trout fishing. Ed has changed my mind about that. The peculiar, unlikely streams within a twenty-minute walk of Andy Snow's, as it turns out, are flush with the most beautiful, iridescent, lively, if wary, native fish. This has made me a fan of local, humble waters.

Last summer, based on a relatively clear set of directions from Ed, my son and I went in search of "the stone bridge fishing spot," the one at which, Ed said, a rather goofy and social black bear once sat on the opposite bank watching him fish. The deer flies devoured Spencer and me on the walk through the woods, but sure enough we located the spot: a beautiful, diminutive pond behind a beaver dam, steeply bounded on all sides by tall spruce trees, ducks gliding among the lily pads in shallow water, the outlet spilling over a boulder walkway, the "stone bridge," below which the stream gurgled its way south. The fish were jumpin' and the water was high. No goofy bear, alas. We fished happily—but unsuccessfully . . . we were *fishing*, not catching— for an hour, and then retreated up the trail as a warm summer rain dimpled the pond. It was worth suffering the deer flies.

It took me a while, but I did finally achieve Ed's actual company for an afternoon of fishing. I offered to be blindfolded and spun around before the walk to the Secret Spot, and he seemed to consider it seriously. And it was a sign of deep trust, I guess, that I was not blindfolded nor even sworn to silence. Or perhaps it was just a sign of the relative value of the spot to which he guided me. This day might have been a test of worthiness. We were beginning on the bottom rung of trout lairs, I suspected. It is a sliding scale.

One sunny day we scouted a small brook, jumping from bank to bank, sneaking up on potential pools so as not to scare the wily brookies. Ed perceived fishy nests in unusual places. We flogged the quick waters, I with dry flies and Ed with a number eight hook and a worm. And it was as if he called the fish by name, the way they came to his lure—fish after fish, each greeted by the Vizier with an affectionate "hello darling," like an old friend, each fish gently returned to its home with a respectful toss. As it turned out, my afternoon was nothing but casting practice. Evidently, there is more to the fishing relationship than being acquainted with the right spot. Native fish respond differently to native fishermen, or is it vice versa. Perhaps Ed knows that. Perhaps this year he will tell me the secret password. There may also be a handshake.

Who Cooks for You?

ON FOUR OUT OF FIVE DAYS during the past two weeks I have had the good fortune to see the same large barred owl in the same place at the same time. It has become an evening rendez-vous. We are both punctual, or at least on the same schedule, and meet up at about 5:00 p.m. Whereas I consider it a daily appointment, I cannot be sure what the owl puts down in his calendar. He is inscrutable.

A stout twelve inches tall, he has mottled feathers and usually sits in one of two trees, a maple or an apple tree, though last night he perched atop a utility pole. Regardless of the perch, he is always surveying the same area, a field the size of a soccer pitch, though he does pause, momentarily, to consider my greeting. I think. It's hard to tell just what an owl is thinking. You do get the feeling, however, that "thinking" is indeed the right word for what he's doing. It's possible he is thinking me rather inscrutable.

The first time I saw any owl was during a walk in the woods last winter. He startled us as he sat on a low branch of one of our maple trees. Who knows how long he had been observing us. He met our gaze with a penetrating stare and then swooped through the cedars when he had finished sizing us up. You certainly do feel looked at by an owl, almost interrogated by its gaze.

I observe my new owl with binoculars. Call it bird watching, but owls do not behave like other feathered species. Their visage is almost human. With eyes on the front of their head, and a beak that is very nose-like between those large eyes, they seem to have a face rather than a beaked profile. They stare you back full faced. They hold your gaze. They spook but are not spooked. It seems that I am conducting the engagement on his terms, and he feels very secure, thank you very much, to depart the appointment at his own convenience.

I've done a little research. The feathers on the leading edge of my owl's wings are serrated, so they do not produce any noise as he swoops downward in the darkness. He is a stealth predator, equipped with phenomenal eyesight and keen hearing, however bulky and un-sleek his airframe.

According to the U.S. Forest Service, "If [humans] had eyes proportional to those of the great horned owl, they would be the size of grapefruit and weigh five pounds each." Owls locate their prey by sound, zeroing in on the hapless field mouse or vole by comparing the arrival time of sounds reaching their left versus right ears. "Who cooks for you" is their radar call.

I spent some time on Saturday morning investigating the field where my owl presides. He was sleeping in. My hope was to find his nest, or at least some pellets beneath one of his perches. My daughter's science teacher would no doubt get a couple of good lessons by investigating the diet of this local owl. Alas, I discovered nothing—and am glad, in a way, not to become too scientific in my understanding of owl life. These are technical distinctions, and to me an owl is more than the sum of its parts.

My preference is to think in mythological terms, and part of my mythology is what I know of owls from A.A. Milne. Before

Harry Potter's mail-carrying owl, Hedwig, came to be the Alpha literary owl, there was Owl. Or "WOL," as he spelled it.

Owl was the go-to sage of 100 Aker Wood, the professor with the pince-nez glasses, the bird with the handsome bell-rope on his stoop. When Eeyore lost his tail, Owl had the plan: "The customary procedure is as follows: First, issue a reward."

In fact, Owl had more information and explanation than Pooh had use for. "Owl went on and on, using longer and longer words, until at last he came back to where he started."

Owl also had Eeyore's tail: that handsome "bell-rope," which he had found hanging from a bush in the forest.

And such is the sense that I have from my owl: that he is, in fact, withholding information, knowing the level of my tolerance for long words and detailed explanations. He knows more than he can say, more than I am prepared to understand. But he is tolerant and encouraging our relationship, or he would not continue to be so punctual. Someday, clutched in his talons, I expect to see a letter addressed to me—or perhaps a button-on donkey tail.

My Thought-Fox

FOUR IN THE MORNING in my mind is a blank page until the dogs insist that something unusual is taking place outside. On the night of the full moon, their ruckus brought me downstairs, peering out the front door at the long-tailed shadow dancing around on the crusty blank sheet of snow.

The dancer was a fox, and it was enjoying the seed-scatter under the bird feeder, digging and nibbling on sunflower kernels left by the brash, greedy blue jays. Or was it pouncing on unsuspecting mice that had tunneled to the same spot for their share of kernels?

A poem was surfacing in my mind. I had observed this scene before as a reader.

> *Through the window I see no star:*
> *Something more near*
> *Though deeper within darkness*
> *Is entering the loneliness:*
>
> *Cold, delicately as the dark snow,*
> *A fox's nose touches twig, leaf;*
> *Two eyes serve a movement, that now*

And again now, and now, and now
Sets neat prints into the snow

"The Thought-Fox," by Ted Hughes, was playing out for real in the forest of my sleeplessness and the tense alert of our dogs. For Hughes, the poem *was* the fox, pawing and sniffing around the corners of his imagination until it finally jumped from the mental verge into verse.

Isn't that just like the month of March, to lurk beneath the bird feeder where the clutter of chickadees has spent all winter, and then suddenly wake the dogs? This soft-furred, sharp-toothed month is an interloper between winter and spring, caramelizing the mud and then stiffening the puddles back to solid winter, loosening up the sap on warm afternoons, and then hardening the arteries with a sudden arctic night—snow days followed by shirtsleeve weather and constantly nipping at our heels. March preys on our yearnings.

The wild things have been on the move for the last week. The dogs and I hold vigil with our chins on the windowsills waiting for something, anything to appear out of the woods. The deer, skunks, and squirrels oblige, and even a fisher cat cruises through our field, piquing the extra-sensory perception of Gus, the big dog. Even if he can't see, smell, or hear them, he knows they are lurking, attending to the wild business of spring. I can at least sense the atmospheric charge.

When the thought-fox moves on, "the page is printed." What comes next? Bears are still slumbering. But if maple trees are making sugar, can the thought-bear, and her cubs, be far behind, ambling across this page toward summer berries?

A Burning Desire

BURNING IS A MAINE RITE of spring. There's something ancient and therapeutic about sending the deadwood from winter tree harvesting up in smoke, spending a day tending a large fire, poking and turning logs and slowly adding fuel, watching the sparks dance against the night sky as the pile reduces itself to embers.

I feel selfish not sharing such an occasion—a burn pile ought to be communal. So, I invited my friend Brian to join me beside yesterday's fire. Henry David Thoreau was there, too.

Early in *Walden*, Thoreau exposes man's possessions as "more easily acquired than got rid of." He then describes the annual burn ritual of the Mucclasse Indians. The villagers gather all their old food and belongings and burn them as an act of cleansing and purification. Then they make a fresh start. Even the fire on the hearth would be started anew from sticks rubbed together by their high priest.

They called it a "busk," according to Thoreau. "I have scarcely heard of a truer sacrament," he writes, "that is, as the dictionary defines it: 'outward and visible sign of an inward and spiritual grace.' We often forget that resolutions may begin with the motive to be different, new. But to be successful, the reformer must make room."

I was inspired to turn my fire into a full-scale busk ritual. Surely here was a ceremonial opportunity for unloading the thousands of pages of clippings, notes, and English teaching morsels I had been lugging around with me over the past twenty years. What more fitting way to make a break from an English major's accretion of stuff—to say nothing of cleaning the basement—than to add my ball and chain of files to the fire. Thoreau would have loved it.

Back to the house and down to the basement I went, where I eyed the three-foot cardboard file box loaded with the "A-through-H" archive.

Should I sort through them, just to make sure that nothing irreplaceable was going up in smoke? But I knew that was a slippery slope. Once I started looking through folders I hadn't touched in five, ten, or fifteen years, I would begin to quibble with myself. If I hadn't looked for those college notes on Sherwood Anderson by now, I never would. If the precious articles on Frost and Fitzgerald and Hemingway that I had so carefully clipped, pending future relevance, had gone unread all these years, were they truly precious?

Deadwood, I decided. Baggage.

Of course, as the Mucclasse Indians knew, the actual collector of all these files and data is no longer around. If I am honest with myself, I must admit that many of the things I thought important twenty years ago seem dusty and old now. I have "been there, done that." Data is static, transitory in value. The collector is dynamic, alive, searching. And each day is a fresh fire of the heat of inquiry and learning.

A through H went on the burn pile in its entirety. It slowly crackled and hissed between the logs and branches. There was something satisfying about this ritual. I went back for I through

S. Good-bye Ibsen, Keats, Milton, *New York Times*, punctuation tests, Restoration comedy, Shakespeare . . . even Thoreau.

Hold on! Here were several very fat folders. Shakespeare took up six inches of file-drawer space. They held numerous plays I had used in my English courses, with critical gems and wonderful writing assignments on each one. This was the Bard, after all. Could I divest myself of the greatest writer in the English language?

Resolved: The Bard lives; my Bard files do not.

Little by little, as the afternoon progressed, ten linear feet of paper files were consumed by my busk ritual. My drawers have been cleansed. I have made room for the new.

This morning I walked out to the ashes. It was sunny, windy, and the first songbirds of spring—the thrush and red-winged blackbird—trilled at the verge of my field. I stirred the embers of memory and noticed a few blackened pages on which I could still recognize some type. The rest is gone, making room for the ritual of new collections, fresh fire. Summon the high priest.

Thrush Hour

"IT IS THRUSH HOUR," I tell my daughter. I step outside to the back porch. We are still just east of twilight. The air is soft. The fir trees are fragrant. I wait all year for these songbird weeks of summer, for this particular songbird, and, each night, for this hour, this listening ritual.

The crows have withdrawn, the robins are nested, woodpeckers fled. The wood thrush in the treetops behind our house, dryad of the coast of Maine, begins its evening coloratura. I hear the rippling grace notes of *pibroch*, so many notes in a fluid arpeggio. They are the birds "whose voices make the emptiness of light / A windy palace."[2]

I press the voice record button on my iPhone hoping to capture this serenade, its next melodic burst. Then I type my thrush hour message, press send. The world is flat. Though Ariel is hundreds of miles away in a suburban enclave *sans* thrush, we can share this song. Ornithological distancing. Imperfect. Merely adequate. And yet, transporting.

I would not appreciate the thrush song so much if my grandmother hadn't taken me into the pine woods behind her 19th-century New Hampshire farm—a weekend retreat—the true family farm was generations previous, many states distant—and taught

---

2. "Thrushes," *Siegfried Sassoon.*

me to listen, then hear, then name, then love this bird. "That's a red-winged blackbird," gramma said. The thrush was the prize. Her face lit up as it trilled. The same bird, same evocative song I heard tonight, here in Maine—gramma's song, texted to her great granddaughter that she never met. Quantum songbird entanglement.

I loved gramma's way of tilting her head to one side at the sound of a bird call, even raucous blue jays. Her gesture was enough to say, "Stop. Listen. That one," singling out the solo bird she wanted me to hear above the background forest chatter. She had the same way with a melodic line in Chopin. She was an accomplished pianist too.

New England birds must have reminded gramma of her childhood spent at Bradford Woods outside Pittsburgh, and the beloved rustic cabins to which her family retreated for the summer. There was a spring-fed swimming pool, fields and woods, dogs and horse buggy, and walks and picnics with cousins—a village of childhoods. I have her old black and white photo albums of the family idylls, peace, play, love, and a simpler time. Her father drove an early Ford in a duster, with goggles. The family had an early box camera and took care to document their life with formal multi-generational portraits and candid snapshots of kids paddling leaky homemade wooden boats. It was the beginning of popular photography, and our family's visual record. Gramma annotated them all. Instagram, circa 1917.

And the thrush? I imagine Gramma walked those hardwood forests with her grandmother Amelia Gerwig, her namesake, singling out the songbirds together, handing off the knowledge and love to the younger generation.

I have the little wooden cabin facsimile that her great uncle carved for her, a scale replica of her own full-size play cabin. It's now a sacred object on my bookshelf, bringing back the vestigial memories of my own childhood visit to those cabins, before suburbia encroached. In the early 1960s, the swimming pool persisted; gramma's little cabin invited us in. Gramma tilted her head as if to stop and listen to the echoing sounds of prior childhoods lingering, for her, in the forest air of what was once called the Northwest Territory by her forebear settlers. Is the thrush song so different from a happy, giggling child?

The song remains the same, across time and the history of American migrations and settlement and heritage, as the listeners of five human generations commune with a single avian species, on a July evening in Maine. "Heard melodies are sweet, but those unheard/Are sweeter."[3]

---

3. "Ode on a Grecian Urn," John Keats.

My Next Bear

HAVING SPENT A LOT OF TIME looking out the back window at home, I've been thinking about bears. Because that's where I saw my last bear crossing my line of sight two summers ago, it is where I expect to see my next bear. I habitually look in that direction every time I peer out the back door. It is a kind of "persistence of vision" that the memory has inscribed on my yearning for another bear sighting. Nor is it accurate to think that every black shadow I see among the fir trees in my woods is a bear. But I do this too.

I know that to see the next bear, I must adapt and expect a sighting when I least expect it, where I least anticipate its appearing . . . just like my prior summer's bear. And the one before that. There will no doubt be experienced bear stalkers who have far finer points to put on my theory and experience. But this is my way of organizing the meaning of my experience. I am constructing Todd's Theory of Bear Apparition.

Reports abound. Sue and Bob saw one on the hill going down to Wadsworth Cove. I was robbed—that was intended to be my next bear. They are from out of town. Social media helps: "Bear by the Colsons!" "Crossing the road toward Blakes!" Do the bears know they are on Facebook? Snapchat? And of course, video from the transfer station where two hapless bears ended up trapped due to a fondness for donuts. Who can blame them?

Then there's the bear poop discourse, thanks to a photo posted from Witherle Woods. "Could this be moose?" Survey says: bear. Full of seeds. Moose is more like deer. Inquiring minds want to know.

Whenever it's time to be on the watch for bears, I think of what Sally said: "A bear is like a black velvet hole in the woods." And in any given patch of woods, there are so many dark spots—stumps and shadows that end up *not* being a bear stepping forth and sniffing the breeze—that when the bear is finally there it takes a minute to realize exactly what you're seeing. *Nah. Wait. It is!*

A bear's mythological character trumps its status as local wildlife phenomenon. Bears are constellations and totems and moods and desires. And are we not bears, as we climb March hill? Spring calls forth a bit of the bear in each of us, including that black cloak that disguises our winter selves to our spring selves, and, for a few weeks, lets us blend in, but also drives us forth, stretching and yearning for April's sun. We must look twice to see our own footprints in the mud. We've come to blend too thoroughly with our emotional winter "woods." We too are hungry, foraging, hanging around bird feeders, and campfires . . . and dreaming of the plump berries to come. And now that they're here, we'll share the bounty with our ursine friends as we all plump up for the next hibernation. Bears: text me next time you're over this way. One selfie—that's all I ask. I've got donuts.

We Will Have Our Syrup

Cold nights, warm days. The forest is speaking to us in sugar.

LONG AGO, DURING A LATE WINTER SKI WEEK in New Hampshire, my father took me down the road to visit Mr. Lucy's sugarhouse. At one time, the Lucy family owned and farmed much of the Saco River valley land on the west side of North Conway, and still lived in the big farmhouse on the West Side Road near our cottage. Their corn fields ran right up to the river and the maple sugar bush on Moat Mountain. The sap was running, and the sugarhouse was fired up, the evaporator running full tilt.

As we peered through the door, there was Mr. Lucy, hoary and bearded, walking through the maple steam like the ghost of Hamlet's father appearing in the gloaming. He beckoned us in and proudly showed off the amber syrup already filling bottles and gallon cans on the workbench.

The dark mystery of the visit comes to mind when the sugar maples start to flow. It is not Whitman's lilacs that augur spring for denizens of this latitude, this type of forest. It is bottles of amber sugar that the trees give us, hope of flowers and raspberries. It beats potholes as harbingers. Syrup time is its own law of thermodynamics.

Many years later, when I was a high school student in a town outside of Boston, a guy named Bill McElwain noticed all the ancient sugar maples in the suburban front yards. Here was a latent resource, now that the old farms had been supplanted by split-levels. Bill was the town Youth Commissioner and could always get a following for a new scheme. He had a twinkle in his eye, most days. He also saw the green power in farming on town land and organized community gardening long before it became commonplace.

Bill had a decrepit, blue Econoline van and a corps of dedicated teenage kids to help hang buckets on those trees—just plastic gallon milk jugs to start with—and run around town collecting the sap each afternoon after school. This led to building a true sugar shack next to the brand new junior high school—funky, rough-sawn boards on a cabin next to the multi-million-dollar, concrete 1960s architectural monstrosity. The evaporator-alchemy absorbed piles of kindling and turned out a golden syrup for sale in recycled mayonnaise jars—instant karma plus youth industry. Bill too looked like Hamlet's father, supervising the evaporator and inhaling maple mists, while his minions stoked the fire and replenished the sap.

Teenage syrupers! As zealous for sap as for wilder, self-centered pursuits—we were a human sugarbush. Making syrup and gardening tapped the spring sugar flowing through us kids. Making vegetables grow or making a magical liquid for pancakes out of nothing but the effort of gathering it, was a great use of other latent suburban resources: me and my friends. And those of us whose vocation is now the schoolyard see the magic come again.

Where can you see elementary school spring sap flowing? The sun is higher and the playground mud thaws and freezes each night. Chewy footing by noon recess, tundra again by midnight. But each day as the kids flow off the bus, their games have an insistent exuberance and zip—bucketloads. Sugar in sneakers. The snow pants are off, and the speed of chasing games moves way up the curve. Green things are poking their heads through the snowbanks. Hannah spotted the daffodils along the west wing foundation, crocuses are up, that faithful cardinal is back from southern climes and you can hear his trill in the elm canopy daily. Somewhere, I like to imagine, Farmer Lucy and Bill McElwain are getting out the buckets and taps and firing up the heavenly evaporator. Maybe the blue van still turns over, running on maple sap vapors. There's no turning back now. We will have our syrup.

Springtide

SPRING IN MAINE is an intertidal zone, a slow, ragged exposure of winter's ravages on the way to summer's fruitfulness and bounty. It is a persistent skirmish between freezing and thawing, hibernation and new birth, torpor and explosive flowering, migration and returns of all kinds. Grumpy bears come out of their dens with new cubs to feed, the peepers and vernal pools evanesce, flowers and berries prepare to nourish. We are betwixt and between and migrating. Cold recedes, warmth timidly floods in. Spring is full of becoming, and we too are its creatures.

Some weeks we feel like mollusks exposed in tidal mud, enticed by brief exposure to stronger sun and milder air. We poke our siphons out of the shell and take a whiff. It's usually a toss-up: retreating is just as promising as stepping up and out. It's not the first time spring will beguile us. Spring is always a tease. Because she can be—she has what we desperately want.

My favorite spring motif is the running of the alewives upstream back to their spawning waters. In May, they arrive in Mill Brook, which meanders from Pierce Pond to the tidal Northern Bay of the Bagaduce River, then down to the mouth of the Penobscot River. They are swimming through a long, shallow gauntlet from their saltwater winter haunts back to freshwater to lay their eggs, as they have done for thousands of years. At one time, most Maine rivers had alewife runs.

Mill Brook has a new fish ladder that eases their return. Some of the alewives have been at sea for a couple of years. It's a big debut. The locals have taken an interest in the anadromous species—giving them a leg up to keep their love life going. It doesn't help with the bald eagles, however, perched overhead streamside. It's a hundred-yard-long cafeteria-style buffet. Fast food. I've counted upward of a dozen eagles at a time, just waiting for the tide to bring alewives into easy reach. Easy pickings. Mealtime. Diner's open. Death from above.

Some days I am the alewife. Some days I am the eagle. I too am swimming upstream toward summer, hiding amidst my brethren, borne back ceaselessly into winter. Or worse, snagged in the talons of a late frost. When I am the eagle, I am an apex predator swooping on any spring opportunity to gorge—on sun, fecundity, breeding, blossoming. Humans, too, want actual alewives to smoke, in time-honored tradition. As local author Cherie Mason explained it, "Everybody is somebody's lunch." Except the eagles. They are no longer an endangered species. I feel I am, if I don't make it to June. I've made it past April. May will not snack on me.

We are almost to the fish ladder, to the pond, to warm, freshwater. Winter's predation wanes. Love stories abound. The vernal pool, the tottering bear cub or fox kit, the tree frogs, even black flies augur better times—respite from cold, dark, isolation and lock-down. The furnace is done, the snowplow man will not be back, winter's final bills can be safely paid. The remaining woodpile now becomes a carryover to next year's heating season. Even the chores of summer, for the time being, are a celebration and glad reunion. Nothing like that first grass cutting on the riding mower and turning over the garden. By the end of the month—not too soon . . . wait for that final May full moon— we might even think about putting the tomato plants into the ground. Always a fickle prospect, here in Maine, where we can barely eke out a true vine-ripened salad by August.

A chain of blossoming commences. Lupines for June graduations, raspberries not far behind, blackberries, then blueberries. The freezer stockpile will be evenly divided between fresh and future pies and shortcake. Summer is about dessert calories. The takeout stand will open for Memorial Day, inaugurating cone season. "Maine's best" signs abound: lobster and crab rolls, onion rings, pie—we've been waiting ever since Labor Day. Gotta dine at the picnic table beside saltwater or it just doesn't count. We eagles savor onion rings too.

We return, we return. We are back. Hunkering down is over. Like the mummer motif of ancient villages, we twirl our ribbons and sing the old songs. Mine goes like these lines from e. e. cummings:

> *sweet spring is your*
> *time is my time is our*
> *time for springtime is lovetime*
> *and viva sweet love*

Yes, we too may originate in the sea; we too may return to its metaphoric embrace—winter. But the vernal tides also toss us up the pebbled shore toward summer on land to find love in the sweet, fresh pond of June.

Summer

Fishin' Blues

I THINK OF IT AS THE SUMMER OF MACKEREL. On the second evening of our vacation in Castine, Maine, my son Spencer caught his first fish, a shimmering black, green and silver mackerel of between twelve and twenty inches in length, depending on the time at which Spencer regaled us with the story. The three kids and I had been hanging around the dock as a school of mackerel chased "baby fish" in to the beach. Several other boys with fishing rods were hauling in a fish with each cast. Spencer, usually reticent, asked the most successful of the fishermen if he could have a cast, and, with the borrowed rod, he promptly caught his trophy.

Or it would have been a trophy if he hadn't been reluctant to have me hit the fish over the head in order to bring it home for dinner. He had a tentative desire to eat the fish but didn't want to "dispatch" it. We tossed it back in the bay and marveled at the delicate wet sequins it left sticking to our hands. That catch was enough to induct him and his sisters into a new pursuit. Within a few days, as Spencer was describing to his uncle David the magnificence of his mackerel, I noticed that he had picked up some of the lingo of the fishermen. "We just fish for sport—we don't eat them," he explained over the telephone line. How did he know what "the sport" was?

It reminded me of my own entry into the hunter-gatherer stage of development. My first important fish, a pickerel, came after weeks of patient tedium at the edge of the neighborhood pond on the other side of "the big woods." I had been pulling little sunfish up out of the shadows beneath lily pads for a long time, but this wasn't truly sporting, as I hardly needed bait to get them on the hook. But one afternoon near dusk I was shocked by that shiver in the rod made by a larger fish hitting the lure. I played the fish, eased it around the logs and weeds, and pulled it up on the gravelly shore. My buddy Jeff told me it was a pickerel, or I wouldn't have known what I had caught. It was somewhere between twelve and twenty inches of sinewy sport fish. It looked to me like a small barracuda.

I threw it in a bag and skipped up the path back home. Mom asked if I wanted to eat it. Fortunately, Jeff knew how to prepare it for the pan and he slit it down the middle, to discover a minnow in its stomach. A baby fish! *It had been pregnant*, I thought. *My pickerel was a mother.* I lost my appetite.

If my kids wanted to fish for sport I could back them up, I decided, and headed off the next day to LaVerdierre's Super Drugstore for rods and reels for all the kids. I selected some mackerel jigs and, the lure of choice in Castine, a Swedish Pimple. There is considerable lore in the naming of lures, I'm certain. The name for what is essentially only a well disguised, hybrid pin must be redolent of not only the lure's submarine action but also the genealogy of great fishermen and of great fishing locales. Thus, we have in our tackle box the likes of the Red Devil and the Jitterbug; the tweedy Royal Coachman, Hendersons, and Grey Wolff for fly fishing; and the mysterious Russian Doll.

And so, we began to fish daily and in earnest, revising our visits to the dock according to tide and probability of the mackerel running. Hilary got the hang of casting with a spinning reel very quickly and would flick the bailer over efficiently, hold the gossamer line with her index finger, and toss her Pimple into the harbor, beckoning the fish with a cheerful "Here ya go, sweeties!" She became a specialist in snagging the small harbor pollock that lurk between the large boats and the wharf. Ariel was the most determined of us all but wasn't too clear on the sport aspect of the endeavor. A three-year-old has a hard time grasping the meaning of the reel; but as long as she was holding a rod over water—this was fishing. Her real preoccupation was inspecting the catch of the day wriggling in the buckets beside successful anglers. Not the least bit squeamish, she enjoyed touching their slick sides and glazed eyeballs.

Spencer and Izaak Walton would have had fun together, for he thought deep thoughts as he flogged the stream. *What do fish do while they sleep,* he mused? He had an epiphany about the phrase "holy mackerel." And I especially liked his poetic instructions to Hilary: "cast into the dark cloud of minnows." While catching fish was the insipient goal of standing on the dock, rod and reel in hand, to Spencer it became more of a pastime, the activity being an end in itself. It was a chance to look astute, nonchalant, even blasé about reeling the writhing chrome minnow through the tide. On some mornings his fishing stance was more reminiscent of playing air guitar than fishing, as he strode the dock with the rod perched over his shoulder and twirled around as he reeled and plucked the line. The lure usually fell to the bottom and snagged the seaweed, creating the illusion of something big and fishy on the line. Many of the fish that got away were nothing more than the seaweed dislodging itself.

Fishing spawns new units for measuring the passage of time. "I'll come home after five more casts," or "I'll just catch two more fish," or "Let's go to the dock when the tide is just short of slack" were the new minutes and hours in the passing of a summer day. It is also the Ahab mindset: there's a fish out there and my next cast will catch it. There can never be a last cast, only the present or the next cast. And so we stand on the dock, cranking our reels, keeping the lure in perpetual motion, always about to catch a huge fish, always just missing a big bite, always seeing in any ripple of wake or tide the Moby flick of a trophy fin.

One day we took a break from fishing to fly our kite at Fort Madison, a series of grassy knolls, former gun emplacements looking seaward. Our kite was catching the gentle breeze blowing up Penobscot Bay and we managed to pay out all 500 feet of line before reeling it back to earth. It struck me, as the three kids, the dog and I watched our shimmering slip of colored nylon, just how much time we were spending in a unified gaze toward the end of a line.

Our lures had just as surely caught us as they had mackerel or July gusts of wind. Caught us, Grandfather Lowell during his visit, Uncle Alain, whom Spencer managed to hook in the back with an errant Swedish Pimple cast, and future hunter-gatherers—we had the whole family on the line, antecedent and descendant. Our photos of the dock in this summer's album—of three kids with poles looking to the water, a three-year-old and her grandfather working the reel, a father tying knots in the slippery 5-lb test line, sons and daughters holding up the catch—could be any generation and many a clan.

By the second week of our vacation the local mothers were complaining that the mackerel were stacked like cordwood in the freezer and they couldn't give away the incoming catches. One kid caught thirty of an evening. We weren't having that problem. We just catch them for sport. No telltale bucket on the dock for the curious to examine. "Fishing's good, but we threw them back," we could say. "Oh, about this big, mostly," we could say.

And this brings us to fish stories. Spencer heard tell of the boy who caught a bluefish, a true sport fish, off the rocks down at Dice Head Lighthouse. He had been reeling in a mackerel when the bluefish made a meal of it and found himself hooked on the mackerel jig. The stunned youngster caught the big fish on very light tackle, having had the intention of catching only mackerel. When we went to the same rocks, I had no such luck. Spencer, however, fishing around the corner and out of sight, came sauntering back with arms spread wide to tell me of the bluefish he had narrowly avoided catching. "It was this big," he gestured expansively, "and you can ask those two guys over there. They helped me land it . . . before it got away." I was proud of his achievement, describing "the one that got away" with such assurance. He even picked up the concept of fishing for a particular kind of fish. Perhaps he had heard me ask a group of people awaiting their fishing charter, buckets of bait fish arrayed on the dock, what they were going after. "We're from Texas," said one woman. "We're after whatever will bite." Soon Spencer would be substituting "tuna" for "mackerel," when asked about his catch.

If the blues were running, I wanted in on the action. I went to the hardware store and got the Russian Doll lure—guaranteed to work on the blues. And so it did. On my first cast I had a small harbor pollock on the hook coming in nicely. Then I felt another tug and more weight—a mackerel had evidently snacked on the pollock. Now I saw how this lure worked. Sure enough, there was a big splash and a jolt on the line as if a Toyota had latched on. This was the bluefish and he was hauling line out of my reel at an alarming rate.

I was worried about anything larger than that sounding to snack on the blue fish, so I needed to land my trophy quickly. I reeled and pulled and gingerly tired the fish out. It was midnight by the time I landed that thing, and no one was left on the dock to see the size of it—or help me to lift it out of the water. I had to turn it loose. There just wouldn't have been room on top of the car to bring that fish home.

The Sounds
of Summer

"THAT IS SUCH A SUMMER SOUND," said my daughter Ariel.

She was helping me to hang the wooden screen door on the front of the house, so she had the privilege of letting it slam for the first time. The hinges creaked, the door swished toward the house, and wood met wood with a clap. Suddenly we were transported to the zone of lazy afternoons, popsicles, and flip-flops, transported to numerous prior houses and neighborhoods, and numerous seasons by this mnemonic of summer.

We are accustomed to summer arriving dressed in longer and warmer days, and sightings of migratory species returning: goldfinches are back at my feeder, the bears are out, new deer are tentatively following their mothers, and summer people are taking the thermometers out of their front windows and airing out the porch furniture. Contractors are picking up the pace to finish winter projects in time for clients' return. Golfers abound.

But I'm noticing that summer arrives more surreptitiously as sounds. The trees will have their rattling voices back, as leaves unfurl and catch the breezes. The peeper choir is pumped up to arena concert volume, and there is a bullfrog near my window that moans about true love nightly at 1:00 a.m. My porch drip edge has a special patter that only spring rain seems to make. Can the annoying whine of the mosquito be far behind? In this aural equinox, even the sound of lawnmowers has a certain welcome auspiciousness—which won't be the case by August.

On our day of proto-summer chores, it was sunny and warm, and the tree buds were itching to rip out on the maple branch. It was time to hang the hammock, and Ariel rummaged in the basement to find where we had stored it last September. Soon we had it strung in its dedicated spot between a fir and cedar tree. The woven ropes clinched tight and the hanging chain creaked on the trees, like rigging flexing under sail—another summer sound. The hammock is always linked to languorous hours with my nose in a book. If summer reading makes a sound, I'm hearin' it. I think I even hear the sound of raspberries "intending to appear," to appropriate a favorite phrase by John McPhee.

Last weekend, you could also hear the lupines growing, the purple blossoms intending to appear. To me, they augur graduation since, by then, we'll be picking them from local fields to make the flower arrangements for the 8th-grade graduation ceremony—where we'll listen to the last songs for this year, and the speeches and tributes delivered in honor of the class ending their elementary school careers.

Our hummingbird feeders are up, and we await our inaugural sighting. But of course, we'll hear them first. Just when I least expect it, there he'll be ferociously darting around the beak of the nectar bottle and fighting off his ruby-throated brethren.

The Fruits of
Our Labors

KERPLINK, KERPLANK, KERPLUNK. Know what I'm talking about?

It is a windy, sunny day in Robert McCloskey country and atop our favorite blueberry picking hill—from which you can see across Eggemoggin Reach to Little Deer Isle, the bridge across the reach to Deer Isle, and Isle au Haut beyond—the berries are finally ripe. We have come to gather food for the winter, like the bears, though our blueberries will end up in muffins, pies, scones, and buttermilk pancakes.

Nonetheless, they will fuel our hibernation. In fact, once our picking starts it will be weeks before we eat a meal that does not include blueberries in some fashion. And the berry density of muffins must not fall below fifteen per cubic inch.

We dream all winter of just such a day on these barrens every time we go to the freezer to take another half quart of the dark fruit for a recipe. These are not high bush, cultivated blueberries, which bear fruit as big as marbles and have little flavor. These berries are the essence of "blueberry." And essence includes working hard for the payoff. To even the energetic pickers in our family, it takes a long time to earn even a mouthful, much less a full quart box. It's not like picking strawberries, or raspberries—a couple of stoops, a few handfuls, and you've got several quarts and can be heading back to the car. Just one quart of wild blueberries will take you thirty minutes to pick by hand, but more likely an hour, since the amount going into the box may pale in comparison with the amount going into your mouth. "One for me, one for you, two for me, one for you," I say to my quart pail. Kerplunk.

A connoisseur of the berry, my wife casts her sharp eye on the corner with the darkest, sweetest berries and makes a beeline for it. The red-leaved bushes draw her to them, and she plunks down amidst several thousand berries within an arm's reach. It is no wonder her quart of fruit has such a luxurious hue: navy blue to our cobalt. She is discriminating, filling her quart berry by berry based on deep color and size. This is total quality management in the blueberry patch. The rest of us go for maximum yield: greatest number of berries per branch per reach. Get the job done, winnow later.

Today is our first foray; we anticipate four more weeks of ripe blueberries. But already our daughters are asking about canning and how they will send berries to friends.

"Can I just wrap them really, really carefully and put them in an envelope to send to Alyssa?" asks Hilary.

"We'll need to seal them in jars," we explain, "or make jam— then you can send them. Otherwise they'll squish. Alyssa would get blueberry paste, not jam."

They want to share the wealth and transmit the joy of this hand to mouth recreation to friends and relatives, and the lack of immediacy is frustrating. They want to package and send the experience they are having. It's a humble food—everyone has tasted a blueberry; everyone can buy them at any supermarket— but the act of harvesting them at the source is exotic. Or perhaps it is the power of the child's connection to eating off the land, much as they delight when they visit a farm. And this is the primal farm: fruit that grows because it belongs here, and always has.

Our youngest daughter, Ariel, said, "I hope some momma bear doesn't mistake me for her cub." She has read *Blueberries for Sal* enough times to know that people and bears must share their blueberry patches on occasion, and if their paths overlap someone must take responsibility for courteously yielding to the creature with prior claim. Today we are the only critters in the patch.

Boxes full, we top off our tummies with a few more handfuls of berries en route to the car. It's hard to stop picking when there are so many left to harvest. And hard to make it all the way home without consuming the profits of an afternoon's work. But there is a homemade ice cream stand at the head of the bay that we pass, and they make an awfully good chocolate chip cone. I must admit, man does not live by blueberries alone.

Beachcombing

BEACHCOMBING IS MY EMBLEM FOR SUMMER. In July, our family lives in a small town on the coast of Maine. We mess around in boats, pick blueberries, fish for mackerel, and lounge bookishly in the hammock by the grandfather elm and traipse along the pebbled shore picking up things. The day ebbs and flows with the tides and daylight, not the clock or the jobs that tick down the rest of the year.

It's not perfectly antique—the harbormaster may be seen wearing an electronic pager and even the tentacles of FedEx reach down the peninsula two days a week. "Here, too, in Arcadia," is found FedEx. I overheard one sailor pleading to her husband, as he headed for the grocery store, "Oh, please don't buy a newspaper." We, too, seek blissful isolation and ignorance. To construct the illusion of 19th-century living, the external world must be kept at bay.

But this is the place for collecting news of our interior world. A section of the shore is a repository for the tides of the bay at the mouth of the mighty Penobscot River, and our harbor the site of several ship sinkings during military skirmishes waged in the 17th and 18th centuries, when world powers vied for access to Maine's forested interior. That's the king's timber upriver—masts for the royal navy. In our first summers here, we had a romantic notion that the worn china and sanded blue glass we gleaned on our shore walks had washed out of a British frigate decaying on the harbor bottom. We felt a bit cheated when we learned that it was only the old town dump sunken a hundred yards out. Our porcelain chips were trash, not treasure. But collecting has not slowed. The children love these humble vestiges of former times. A shard of china painted with blue filigree, or a clay pipe, remains exotic. "Treasure" is defined by provenance and the current collector and is not intrinsic.

Summer's intertidal zone collects and gathers us as much as we collect and gather what the tides deposit. My hammock reading yielded this thought: "A child comes to the edge of deep water with a mind prepared for wonder," writes the late E.O. Wilson. "He is like a primitive adult of long ago, an acquisitive early Homo arriving at the shore of Lake Malawi, say, or the Mozambique Channel."

And so, each summer when we arrive at our deep-water haunt, we begin a new collection to add to the old, examine the effects of winter storms on our Maine Malawi, note the new moorings and new boats and new boaters. We reconnect with people—the watercolor painter, the poet, the retired architect, and the merchant marine engineer. But it is really ourselves with whom we reconnect: picking up where we left off and noticing the significant ways in which we have changed, and the significant ways in which we have not.

Jars of beach china line our mantel; the new album of summer photos helps to chronicle our combing. Against the consistent background of the cove the foreground shows us holding hands with children who walk in taller and taller shoes. The lad who balked when setting foot in the canoe last summer, goes on a long paddle around the pond to see the loons. His sister now fishes solo on the dock when the word goes out: "The mackerel are running." From year to year the changes seem immense, but the snapshots also remind me of the imperceptibility of summer's nonlinear growth, without a scheduled goal or level of achievement to prod or measure. Professor Wilson notes, "Adults . . . undervalue the mental growth that occurs during daydreaming and aimless wandering."

September floods in like a high tide and we return to our alternate rhythm: metropolitan suburbia. As we drop our young beachcombers off at the schoolhouse door, the moment contains complex overlapping of what they were, are, and will be. Languor and aimlessness give way, with melancholy, to organization and structure. But I always hope the kids will retain what they have found by the sea—the daydreams that were the vessels of this summer's collecting—to guide their walk toward June and the next season of beachcombing, of aimless, important wandering. As e.e. cummings wrote,

> *For whatever we lose (like a you or a me)*
> *It's always ourselves we find in the sea*

Manual
Boating Bliss

I DECIDED *not* to buy the five-horsepower outboard motor for my canoe, thanks to Paul. It was a close call. Disaster averted. As we sat on the bakehouse porch Sunday, surveying the early morning harbor, he offered well-reasoned dissent from my notion. Boating perfection, he stated, consists of a canoe, the paddle, and nothing involving internal combustion engines or fuel aside from bakehouse muffins. Why mess with perfection?

I reviewed my sworn allegiance to owning no boat that I could not lift onto the roof of my car—a defense against the occasional hankering for bigger and faster watercraft—and I wish to never enslave myself to boat maintenance. We have ample examples in town of people mortgaged to their large wooden boats, in more ways than one. A large boat cries out for both constant use and constant upkeep, inversely proportioned. No thank you. It's enough just getting the downstairs vacuumed and sorting the laundry for a family of five.

Paul, being an expert in resource conservation and retrieval, and a marine engineer licensed for unlimited tonnage, was accustomed to going to sea on vessels whose engine horsepower was measured in the tens of thousands. Talk of the five-horse outboard on the stern of a canoe was a red flag, a slippery slope. He pointed out how much more pleasure he derives in the torque of a well-wrought wooden paddle single-handedly plying the waves, even against the tide.

Paul doesn't even need to put his canoe on top of the car. He loads it on the two-wheeled garden cart and walks it down Main Street to the landing. No petrochemicals involved. Fuel: a few blueberry muffins will suffice. To Paul's way of thinking, just paddling from the town dock to the yacht club dock and back, down in the harbor, is a quality journey.

Nonetheless, the allure of going farther faster had spurred my rationalization of a small motor attached to the stern. On the big lakes, I reasoned, with the canoe full to the gunwales with tent, stove, sleeping bags, large dog, we would extend our reach by moving at six or seven miles per hour rather than one or two.

"But why go to the big lake? You know that marshy area as you head up toward Hatch Cove? There's nothing like drifting in there and just sitting . . . or going over to Ram Island and getting mussels off the shoals. That's all you need," he mused.

He could probably back it up with an amortization of motor purchase price over time, given frequency of three-hour drives to the big lake, cost of oil and gas for car and outboard, etc. Why work so hard to make the money to buy the engine to get there faster and miss all that there was to see along the way? It's the quality of the journey, after all. I think he knew he could show some restraint; the Thoreauvian arguments held sway. They always do.

There's enough dissuasion in a brief perusal of the boat section of *Uncle Henry's*. Somehow the ads for motorboats serve to chill the experience of boating: too much money, too much fuss, too many numbers and figures involved in getting to know your boat. And no lineage. They are all too far out on the lateral branches of the boating family tree. Why not stick with the original?

John McPhee's thorough research in *Survival of the Bark Canoe* proves my point: with a few simple adaptations, the canoe serves all purposes. "A canoe with a curving, rocker bottom could turn with quick response in white water. A canoe with a narrow bow and stern and a somewhat V-sided straight bottom could hold its course across a strong lake wind. A canoe with a narrow beam moved faster than any other and was therefore the choice for war."

My canoe is narrow in the beam and bow with a bottom responsive in white water and it holds a straight course if I have a good paddler in the bow. It is a Penobscot, a name redolent of old bark designs. A Penobscot Indian of 1750 would see my canoe and know what it is, what it was designed to do, how to paddle it. And he would see no need to peruse *Uncle Henry's* for anything more. This is the ultimate.

Of course, McPhee's is a rather functional treatment of a canoe's specifications and omits the aesthetics of the craft. A canoe is a perfectly proportioned shape, but also a feeling as right as a sonnet. There is an octave of sounds: water lapping at the bow, the suctioning funnel in the water after a strong stroke, pounding of the bow leaping the crest of a rolling wave and landing in the trough, drumming of the paddle on the gunwale as I reach forward to pull the canoe forward, marsh grass combing the bottom on the way to Hatch Cove, and the sound of nothing but my own breathing when the lake or pond is glassy still.

It's fair to say that Paul had done a worthy job consulting with me on my resource retrieval—I only realized later how economical his approach had been. He saw the impending disaster and resource deficit and moved quickly to stanch the flow. I'd love to have him as my bow man the next time we float with the tide from the town dock down to the yacht club and back, or venture to Ram Island for mussels, a roundtrip voyage that will pass many a wooden boat sapping the resources of people who began with a canoe atop their car. Then things went sadly awry.

Echoes of Our Family's Farms

IT WAS A GENTLEMAN'S FARM: ninety acres of woods, vestigial pasture, orchards, a 200-year-old pre-colonial house with ell and enormous, mysterious barn, and a hand-pumped well. At least it felt so to my nine-year-old sensibilities. My nostalgia persists for the creaky wide planks of the uneven floorboards, the perfume of old pine, musty wallpaper and horsehair plaster. The Glenwood stove in the ell was a cherished fascination, the key to hours of fanciful play, pulling Play Doh pies in and out of the iron oven, pretending to stoke the fire box, and lifting the burner plates with the special tool. Grandma loved to explain the significance of the farm's other rustic technology. There were the radiating properties of the shallow fireplaces, the copper bed warmer, the hiding niche behind the massive chimney. One wall of artifacts was a museum: horseshoes, cross-cut saw, stovepipe hat, bear trap, powder horn, Civil War bayonet, canteens, old snowshoes—all treasures found in the house when Grandma and Grandpa bought the property in the 1950s. This was not the family farm; it was its echo.

Grandpa was the gentleman, an insurance executive in Boston. By the time my mother was in college, he and Grandma wanted a retreat where they could indulge in a pastoral pace, woodland songbirds, and visits from the anticipated grandchildren. It worked. Grandma introduced me to the song of the thrush on walks through the spruce forests. The farm yielded the pleasures of handwork like scything the field, chopping wood, even pumping water from the well, a far remove from downtown tools and work—the world of sales, actuarial tables, pencil pushing, and working on commission. It reclaimed for Grandma her childhood summers at Bradford Woods, the country retreat from Pittsburgh where her father ran the family canned food business.

I scratched a little deeper to uncover our roots. As with most American families, the last real farmer was not too distant along any branch of ancestry. My great-great grandfather, Spencer Colby, was the third generation to farm in Moose River, Maine. Life was hard in Moose River. Following the Civil War, Spencer went by covered wagon to Kent County, Michigan. In 1869, he wrote to his brother Helon: "You say that you have an idea of buying more land at Moose River, but my advice is for you to come west. . . . This is a good country for wheat, corn, and grass and stock raising and a great place to raise fruit such as apples, peaches, pears, plums, and tame cherries and most anything you may want to raise." Two Colby brothers ventured west, to Michigan and then farther on to Nebraska. And then, apparently, we got out of farming.

In a turn-of-the-century photo, taken in their yard in Marquette, my great grandfather, Walter Colby, stands beside my grandmother. They live in town, not on a farm. She is seven and holds her favorite doll. Both she and her doll look very similar to a current line of historically accurate dolls that come complete with authentic American stories. And this is how my daughters connect with our family's immigrations, farms, booms, and busts. It is also participation in the societal yearning for links to stories of forebears. Such "song lines" of personal culture are commercialized in a manner alien to the soul of the stories, ironically. But it perpetuates a public intergenerational storytelling that is on the wane within families, just like the family farm.

Walter Colby's children's children mirror America's evolution away from agriculture toward factory work, suburbanization and fewer people per generation. Whereas Spencer and Josephine Colby had twelve children, I have three. We have not earned our living working the land for three generations. A backyard tomato glut will be as close as I come to growing food on my "north forty." We do, however, view our agrarian heritage with curiosity and wonder. I would love to raise up "tame cherries," peaches, and pears on land I call my own. There abides a deep feeling of power in owning land. The lore of the family farm persists. Though my kids never knew Grandpa's farm, they feel an emotional connection to land. We understand "farm" in aesthetic terms; we do not have Spencer Colby's experience of farming as long days full of repetition, struggle, and danger. It is the pleasure of a romantic attachment.

Any of our ancestral pastures must surely have succumbed to metropolitan sprawl and the commuter life. That ninety acres owned by an insurance executive is within striking distance of metropolitan careers and probably the site of a subdivision: colonial reproductions complete with faux ells and garages imitating old barns. The John Deere riding mower takes over the hand scything. All of which makes me grateful to have explored the land at a time when I could still breathe a vestige of its pioneer use—enough to pass along a little lore to my children about family, the song of the thrush, and farms where you could raise "most anything you want to raise."

Inspiration Found on the Writing Road

FOUR DAYS A WEEK, I drive thirty rural miles to my job as an editor. My route takes me past farms, forests, blueberry barrens, saltwater coves and salt pond inlets as well as the Northern Bay Market, C & G Growers and Albert "Bim" Snow's garage, though Bim has closed his shop and retired. The trip is never the same two days in a row, as some feature of the landscape has always been altered overnight or some new feature has emerged for scrutiny: A pothole has been filled, a tree felled, or an osprey comes winging over the road clutching a fresh alewife at the exact moment I round the corner.

But there is one landmark I eagerly anticipate for the fact that it looks the same every day—and has for many years. It's the forty-acre saltwater farm on Allen Cove on Blue Hill Bay to which E.B. White, having "evacuated the city house" in New York, led his family "like a daft piper."

Here they lived with Fred, the dachshund with a "dainty grimace," and Joel, their boat-struck son. White, an aspiring farmer, kept chickens, geese, pigs, a cow, parented baby robins, and, presumably, became acquainted with the large gray spider who came to be known as Charlotte. White had an aunt named Charlotte who once told him, "Remembrance is sufficient of the beauty we have seen." I'd like to think that I have shared the rural view behind those words.

As I rumble by the White place from the north, the cedar hedge, like a crenellation fortifying the front yard, allows me a few glimpses of the orchard, the flower and vegetable gardens, and the central structures: the white, eleven-room federal farmhouse and surrounding sheds and barns. They are in perfect trim, looking exactly as they did in the photos that show Mr. White conversing with his geese or crossing to the chicken coop on a sunny day in mid-winter, as he goes about the day's chores. To use one of White's own phrases to describe revisiting an old haunt, it seems to me as if "there had been no years."

Allen Cove is where White moored his beloved sloop, *Martha*, built in the boatyard Joel would establish nearby, a boat without amenities, not even a depth finder—"I plan to find my depth by listening to the sound the centerboard makes as it glides over the ledges," he wrote. Some years he hemmed and hawed about whether to put *Martha* in the water at all, but he seemed to feel that, regardless of his growing tentativeness about sailing single-handedly, the boat needed to be launched as a sign of hope or aspiration, if not concrete intention.

It takes but seconds to drive past the White farm, but it allows enough of an observation to serve as my daily editorial fillip. Arriving at my writing desk a few miles south of the farm, ready to check my email and go to work with my Mac PowerBook (just imagine the fun White would have had with the term PowerBook!), I feel catechized with his first commandment of usage in *The Elements of Style*: "To form the possessive singular by adding 's." I have come to hear a spare, Down East beauty in the phrase, like a whiff of salt air or an accent behind the counter at the general store.

Here among the farm buildings is the shed in which Mr. White sat and thought and pecked out squibs and essays for *The New Yorker* and *Harper's* magazines. Photographer Jill Krementz captured him in this shed. In her black and white portrait, he sits at a bare wooden table, backed by rough boards, framed by a view to the cove beyond—one man and his typewriter, facing down the blank page, composing sentences that, no doubt, "omit needless words."

The image reminds me of the only essential tools of the trade: the urge to say something true, solitude, lack of distraction, and the means to record words, no doubt working "from a suitable design." He said, "The whole problem is to establish communications with oneself," which hints at the contemplative coves he sailed, above and beyond fussing with comma splices tangling the halyard of the sentence line.

In his writing shed, White felt he was a "wilder" and "healthier man." The shed is about the size of Henry David Thoreau's cabin, the New England naturalist being White's greatest writerly muse and intellectual mentor. They shared a birthday. "What seemed so wrong to Thoreau," White wrote, "was man's puny spirit and man's strained relationship with nature." He urged the Thoreauvian tactic of taking time to "observe and feel." On the Maine farm, White found himself "suddenly seeing, feeling, and listening as a child sees, feels, and listens . . . a time of enchantment."

And so, I check in on the White homestead much as White checked in on Thoreau and himself, and I am reminded of the comments White wrote to introduce a new edition of *Walden*, with photographs by the naturalist Edwin Way Teale. In the book, he said, readers can "hear one naturalist speaking to another across a hundred years." It's a pretty good dose of inspiration from a modest bend in the road. The remembrance is indeed sufficient to make me see, feel, and listen with new-old senses.

Sign of the Times

THIS IS ABOUT A NEW STORE SIGN, and how the one it replaced was auctioned off for the benefit of the volunteers of the fire department and ambulance service a few years ago. But first, you need to get a sense of the scene.

Castine is the sort of small town store where it would not be out of the ordinary, on a particularly busy August day, to find Joe Slocum, the town manager, pitching in to wash dishes behind the counter, Carl Raymond, the retired fireman, filling the soda cooler with fresh bottles, or various customers coming and going and filling out their own slips for video rentals. The Variety gets busy.

For instance, Janis and Big Ernie, the proprietors of the Variety for the past ten years, since Janis's mother Gail retired, scoop the most Gifford's ice cream in the state of Maine. That's as good a measure as any of just how hectic things can get.

Paul Manning, a marine engineer who used to work for Mobil and is now self-employed, can explain the Gifford's phenomenon. He is the inventor of Manning's Frozen Confection Coefficient. Putting his engineering expertise in the service of ice cream lovers, he explains to Ernie's customers that the Gifford's is super-chilled, even to the point at which the number of calories required to warm the ice cream for digestion balances the number of calories digested. Hypothetical net calorie intake:

0. Therefore customers feel free to add a second scoop. Actual net income gain for Ernie: 100%. Win-win. Above the counter hangs this sign: "Without ice cream, life would be darkness and chaos."

Paul Manning has also been used by a watercolor portraitist as the likeness for a large painting of the Baron de Castin, the French baron who inhabited these shores in the 17th century. But that's another story.

Ernie and Janis have been *Bangor Daily News* dealer of the month and do a land office business in Eggs McJanis virtually every morning of the year.

Another measure of their importance is the fact that the phone, which jangles all day long, will often ring with a query from someone somewhere in town seeking the whereabouts of their son or daughter, members of the town crew, or even just to check on the tide. Janis and Ernie tend to see everyone and everything, in one way or another, in the course of their day. Their vantage point also works in reverse: Janice called us once to say that Gus, our dog, was wandering the intersection of Main and Water Street. Evidently, he hadn't seen which route we'd taken back up the hill to home and was awaiting instructions.

Sitting on the counter stool the other day, I witnessed Carl using Ernie's call-waiting service: "If anybody wants me, I'll be over at the judge's place," he told Ernie, paying for his green apple soda and heading out the door.

And so Big Ernie's Castine Variety, as the sign and the T-shirts say, is the hub, the crossroads of town. And in this town, all roads, literally and figuratively, lead to the Variety.

Ernie, who used to be in law enforcement (his father was sheriff of Hancock County), arrives by 4:30 in the morning to rev things up. Janis follows later, closer to the time Katie, their daughter, is due at school. And for the rest of the day they preside over the meals, snacks, infotainment, and networking of the town of Castine, Maine.

But the other day, Ernie and Janis made news.

Traffic stopped when their old sign was removed by David Hatch and Ernie Jr., who had erected scaffolding at the corner entrance to the store in order to make the exchange. In a town where change usually occurs in subtle ways—at the speed of paint peeling—this was an abrupt shift. And this was not to be a refurbishing of the old sign, but an updating: the new sign had a revised pictorial theme.

The old sign had hung in place for ten years. It was painted by Ernie's sister-in-law, Pattie Fitch, who runs the variety store over in Surry. It had a classic mercantile emblem, neatly lettered, arranged and weathered to a soft patina at the hands of the salt air and deep cold. On one side the lighthouse at Dice Head. On the other Fort George, which is not much more than some grassy hummocks. To a Castinian, though, the sign is an object worthy of the Smithsonian, given its prominence and centrality to the town.

Suzie Fay, the portrait painter and fiddler who runs the art gallery next door to Ernie's Variety, created the new sign. On the downhill side is a reproduction of the lighthouse at Dice Head. On the uphill side, though, is the town common, complete with yellow school bus in front of the school, and several kids playing on the grass around the Civil War monument, Gus presiding. The big black dog spends many hours per day making sure the squirrels stay up in the elm trees and checking in on the playground while school is in session. When playground balls go missing, the kids search our front yard first.

As soon as the old sign had been removed, Paul Fallow, a volunteer fireman and carpenter, recognized its value as an artifact. Ernie was approached with an offer to buy it, which awakened him to the notion of a benefit auction. It didn't feel like personal property, the sign having been such a significant reference point in the lives of the public, hence his decision that the proceeds would be split between the two volunteer services in town.

The bidding started at $80 and was recorded on a sheet of notebook paper kept on the counter, soon punctuated with various and sundry food stains in addition to handwritten bids. In short order, bidding was leaping ahead at $50 increments. Paul Fallow tried to keep up but dropped out at $650. Below the coffee stains, the bidding finally topped $800, thanks to a Mr. Tom Buchanan. Then it paused. A magic number had, evidently, been reached, and for one week the conversation turned to likely final bidders and their gambit for bringing the sign on home. Who would it be, and what would become of the sign? Would the winner keep it? Donate it to the historical society? Hang it on the wall at the Variety?

Wanda, who frequently worked the counter for Ernie, seemed certain she knew the bidder with the highest motivation, but wouldn't reveal any names until after the final bell, set for 5:00 p.m. on the fifteenth of August. Patrons of the Variety anticipated a frenzy—that was not to be. The final bid rose to $875; the sign went to David and Linda, new owners of the Lowell house on the town common.

True to Manning's Coefficient, the bidding seemed to have consumed pretty much all the available calories, and the volunteer services saw the net gain. It'll be the talk of the town for a week or so before the resumption of the usual topics: the retired skippers' race, the start of school, the first frost and plowable snow, the price of lobster, and Ernie's call-forwarding.

We Come Home
to the Forest

JUST BEFORE THE EXCAVATOR rumbled up the dirt road and began digging the pit that would become our new basement, I paused at a stark realization. *This land will never be the same again.* An unanticipated feeling of tragedy loomed.

We had first become acquainted with our twenty acres of forest land during the winter, walking among the cedars and old apple trees, plodding through snowdrifts, following the deer trails up to the hill in back where the tallest white pines grow. We loved the varied tree growth, the clearing in which we envisioned a large garden, once we overcame the encroaching alder, and the blueberry-covered knoll. Even the marshy lowland seemed enticing while frozen.

All that spring and first summer of land ownership, as we cooled in the cedar shade, picnicked, or slept under the stars, we grew more appreciative of the essence of our location: solitude, privacy, birdsong, animal habitat. Even the coyotes—startling me awake in the tent one night at 2:00 a.m.—were lovable.

But from the start, as we explored the land, it was with an eye toward siting a house, toward inhabiting these woods that had yet to know a human dwelling. Though an 1870 map shows our land as a Perkins family farm—the mossy stone walls, vestigial orchard, and plow layer in the soil attested to that—no one with long local memory remembered there ever having been a house or structure. Ownership has changed hands many times in the intervening years, but there is no fieldstone foundation or remnants of a hand-dug cellar hole.

We got out the compass and thought about sunrise and sunset light. We plotted from the point of view of sitting on a porch for breakfast or watching birds and listening to the spring peepers down in the swamp. We imagined ourselves becoming fellow inhabitants of the land, not just the frequent visitors we had become.

What I didn't imagine was how building a house would change everything about our relationship to the land. Then the excavator began scooping out our cellar hole.

It made sense of some lines by Wallace Stevens:

> *I placed a jar in Tennessee,*
> *And round it was, upon a hill.*
> *It made the slovenly wilderness*
> *Surround that hill.*

I have never been to Tennessee. But was our foundation in Maine like the jar, a form not found in nature about to make this land conform to its specifications? Stevens added a chilling thought, "It took dominion everywhere."

Or was the poem now making sense of the impact our house would have on the land. Was our house about to diminish the very thing that attracted us to our land? Would it dominate the setting that we loved in its pristine—"slovenly!"—state?

As our log home grew in size and impact over the fall and winter, it seemed alternately huge or small. Our perspective changed as course upon course of beams were added, the ridge beam went up, the roof was shingled, windows and doors filled openings and—best of all—the thirty-foot-long front porch was covered. The porch, in fact, seemed like the whole reason to even have the house, since from the start it was the designated spot for just sitting and observing. It would be like an extra room: not inside the house, *per se*, and not fully outside. It was to be our vantage point from which to conduct interactions with that "slovenly wilderness."

There is another aspect to the anecdote of our cellar hole. When you place a "jar" in land with a high-water table surrounding your hill, you may find yourself contending with an unforeseen flow down in the furnace room. Neither the man who did our excavations, nor Stevens, mentioned the possibility of comeuppance by the wilderness: sump pumps in two corners of the basement and a lot of time and consternation spent on the problem of drying out the floor.

However, now that we are moving into our house, it is the pleasure at finally realizing our imagined vantage points that makes it all worthwhile. I can finally sit on my front porch and gaze at the oak and maple trees out front, their leaves just budding out, listen to the peepers among the cattails, spy on the red squirrels in the fir trees taunting our dog, and wait for deer and fox to infiltrate the field at dusk. And my daughter can stare through her roof window at the stars while lying in bed at night. And we can hear the coyotes and owls celebrating at midnight.

I must be satisfied that our dwelling will eventually harmonize with the landscape. After all, the house is a stationary object. The forest is dynamic: it is already growing back and will, in time, restore its serene, original character. Our house may one day grow mossy and hidden, like those Perkins stone walls. An initial sign of reconciliation is the fact that five robins have begun constructing nests in the rafters of our porch. Apparently, a good home is a good home, whether a tree branch or a man-made cabin.

Preserving a
Way of Light

THE LAST LINE OF THE ACCOMPLISHMENTS listed by the town manager in the annual report read, "Brought thirty large elm trees over 100 miles to supplement our stock." When I read it, I flashed back to the day in October when Joe Slocum, the town manager, pulled up in his van, obviously elated.

"I just planted eighteen young elm trees," he beamed.

I imagined saplings, but Joe described twenty-foot-tall trees, each with a root ball weighing half a ton. They'd arrived on an enormous flatbed truck, which made sense of another recollection: Joe with the town crew unloading an elegant tree into a deep hole in a front yard on Main Street. Their joy was obvious, hefting a new tree into a spot left elm-less for quite a few years.

The gap created by an expired elm affects the facade of a house like a missing front tooth. Colonial-era dwellings, with their shady elms planted symmetrically out front generations ago, just don't seem to smile when their trees are gone.

Joe's pleasure in planting something made sense, too. Many of his days are devoted to fixing broken things, planning to fix broken things, or scouting for things that will soon break and need to be fixed: water mains, paving, drainage ditches, heavy equipment, street signs, community relations. Therefore, fixing elm gaps must be especially satisfying, a municipal improvement so obvious and enduring that no one can object.

Who wouldn't take pride in planting any old new tree? But elms are special trees and this small village in Maine is known for them. The majestic old trees dominate Castine. While this once-abundant species has all but vanished from the New England landscape, our elms persist, each tree pampered to thwart the beetle-borne elm blight. Each tree possesses such individual character that they are practically honored with family names. As the town's eldest citizens, they are accorded the greatest respect. Elms have a stature above and beyond that of other trees. Elms preside.

Nonetheless, even here in elm Arcadia, the grand trees are less plentiful than they once were, and there is no younger genera-tion of this species coming along to assume the throne. Photos from yesteryear record the town common with dozens of the graceful trees, planted in strict rows down and across, a regiment of elms.

At the dedication ceremony for the Civil War monument in 1887, the dour citizenry gathered beneath the elm canopy. When I study the photo, it tells me precisely what the light and air must have felt like on that day in May. And I can step outside and experience the same light and air, because it feels the same way on May afternoons in my era.

Though there are fewer trees now, the fewer trees are 100 years larger, their panoply of shade more extensive. I would also say that the contemporary citizenry is much less stern. Like the trees, however, the town's population has shrunk. Today, a dour expression is reserved for losing an elm tree.

The elm in front of my house had a girth as big as the ring made by three of our children plus one adult holding hands, which means it must surely have been planted back when Maine was a British colony. My daughter's 7th grade science class took its measure more scientifically. Its circumference is sixteen feet. They calculated that, allowing nine annual growth rings per inch, the tree had been a sapling planted in 1761.

Alas, it was a few years later when this massive elm had to be removed. I requested a "cookie" of its trunk and mounted it in the timber frame science cabin behind the school. It occupies a whole wall, almost like a rose window. The kids can now end-lessly imagine the historical moments plotted along its annual rings. It is a worthy afterlife.

"They're not easy to paint," said an artist who had been moving his easel around town last August, painting portraits of houses overhung with elms. "There's something unusual about their light and shadow; it's hard to get right." It's the hazy softness of elm foliage, dappling sunlight like yellow-and-green chiffon. These seacoast elms host lichens and mosses that give them a hoary, wizened feel, especially when fog tiptoes off the harbor and adheres to their leaves and branches. I love the feeling of a foggy afternoon when condensation drips from the elms through the cottony air, also the acme of Castine. When the moon rises, it flits through elm branches like a snowy owl hunting mice.

Perish the thought that elm light and shadow are on the wane, soon to be confined to paintings by artists who could get it right, the way Dutch Master studies of rooms in Amsterdam preserve what Renaissance light was like.

So, it's hopeful to see Joe planting elms. It is preventive main-tenance of heirloom sunlight, preservation of the elm shade 100 years hence, regeneration of the canopy for future citizenry assembling on the common on May afternoons.

Inspired by Goldsworthy

BROOKE AND I WENT ON A CANOEING EXPEDITION with Andy Goldsworthy.

Brooke is my brother-in-law; Goldsworthy is the Scottish artist best known for stacking rocks into gravity-defying cairns on the shore of seas and lochs, stitching leaves together with thorns to make an improbable brocade of natural colors, and painstakingly freezing ice arches over streams on chilly highland nights. Many of his works exist only as a photographic record.

Goldsworthy joined our trip in spirit—and that was full participation indeed, as it turned out.

Brooke and I had paddled across Hatch Cove to the first island in the tidal bay of the Bagaduce River. We wanted to explore the ancient hand-dug well and collect artifacts. Osprey and eagles soar above the oblong island, and raccoons, bear, and deer traipse across the mussel shoals at low tide, leaving crab and urchin shells from their meals beneath the oak trees. On a previous visit, I had found an enormous osprey wing feather. We hoped for a similar trophy on this trip.

But we had been looking at photos of Goldsworthy's work in the natural world—and so, instead of collecting feathers, we found ourselves in the grip of the inspiration to make art from found objects while the tide receded. No forest walk, much less a stroll in the park, can be the same after seeing Goldsworthy's "take" on the sculpture embedded in the natural world. When you walk with his insight, you come to a new understanding of art, nature, and inspiration. Therefore, Brooke and I found ourselves in the intertidal zone of possibility and opportunity.

I wondered, for instance, how hard it would be to stack some of the smooth, barnacle-encrusted granite on the pebbled shore; how hard it would be to imitate Goldsworthy and leave something for the tide to nibble and grate at on its return.

I discovered the sleight-of-hand by which you can balance impossibly large stones on their nose: use small pebbles, even sand. Chinked and wedged under the ledge of an overhanging rock, the small stones and granules disappear and create the impression of great weight gingerly balanced on the head of a barnacle. Stone upon stone can follow until a tower presides over the beach with improbable equilibrium. The resulting statue takes on the feel of weights airborne. The heft of big, stolid rocks lifting and reaching skyward. At such an invitation, the beach stones begin asking to dance.

I quickly erected three portly, bottom-heavy dancers, of varying heights, which resembled so many men stomping up out of the water for air. Or, as the tide crept in, slinking back to the depths from whence they came—a devolutionary parade back down to the lobstery, mucky bottom.

Brooke found his artistic license among mussel shells, flat granite, and beach grass. He discerned a kind of mandala in the arrangement of the iridescent shells against a light granite background, fenced in by a prairie of green grass stalks. He created another array, as if the mollusks had been surprised, while in a powwow or tattoo, and were scurrying for cover.

Then Brooke found the seaweed. The photographic record will show him wearing a shaggy headdress of rockweed, a shawl and skirt of kelp fronds. He had fully merged with his medium, the wild man of the Bagaduce sprouting organically from the dark rocks.

We had organized nature, detected a few of the unheard melodies and design aspirations of dumb rocks—or had it organized *us* to receive those melodies to which only an artist's antennae are sensitized?

There is, of course, a certain silent, phantom, six-hour cadence to art concocted in the intertidal zone between high tides. As Goldsworthy knows, when the sun comes up on his ice-sheet bridges, their minutes are numbered; the tide will surely and slowly dismantle my dancing cairns. Perhaps there is a note of sadness in these effects of time and tide, but I would prefer to feel that herein lives part of the artistry: a renewal of possibility and opportunity, in synch with the ebb and flow of creativity. We were responding *with* the landscape, not merely *to* it.

My Bagaduce island cairns are a performance, after all. They stood for a while, as sentinels to curious paddlers flowing past, up and down stream, like Easter Island stone heads stranded in mid-stride. For one tidal cycle they enacted my sense of their potential grace and poise, before snuggling back down, boulder to boulder, in their enactment of underwater "rocky-ness."

We paddled away from the island in the afternoon, leaving our cairns and Goldsworthy mandalas to the elements. But when we got back to the driveway at home, a new inspiration was waiting. The stone wall in front of our house had a different look to it—or we had a different view of it. These stones, too, wanted to dance. So, we set to work stacking them into a stone arabesque.

Awaiting Bear Number Three

BEARS COME IN THREES, I think, though perhaps this is just the conditioning of folklore. Nonetheless, I know that my third bear is in the area and will visit soon.

I was not expecting my first bear. In fact, it seems to be a rule of bears that they will appear when you least expect them. They are just suddenly, sublimely there. So, when my first bear loped across the road in front of my truck one spring morning as I drove to work, I had to pinch myself to be sure I realized that there was indeed a bear there.

No doubt, he was the real McCoy: black bear, in a hurry, and not too concerned with the guy behind the wheel of the blue pickup truck. Bears may be shy, but they are not terribly subtle. He, or she, was beautiful, however, with a coat like a black silk suit, shimmering in the early light, and melting into the dark hilltop grove of fir trees on the south side of the Dunbar road.

I presumed he was on a jaunt to the Narrows searching for food, since it was early spring and the pickings for bears in the fields and forest were still slim. The shores of the Bagaduce River, however, might yield some interesting snacks, and the Narrows was a fast-flowing spot between two bays rich in fish and mussels.

Several years after bear one, my neighbor, Paul Cyr, mentioned seeing a bear at the same exact spot, leading us to wonder just how habitual bears might be in their roaming.

My second bear showed up at six in the morning last May. We had been living in our new house only about a month, and my wife and I were having breakfast in the den. Something dark caught my eye. It was moving. Sure enough, a black bear was walking leisurely through the cedars and across our leach field not twenty feet from the house. He was not the least bit concerned about stealth or disguise.

"Bear!" I exclaimed and jumped for the camera. Alas, no film. Binoculars were handy. We had to content ourselves with observing—and being observed. Bear two sniffed around the woodpile out back, lifting his head up over the top log to peer at his audience. Then he decided to saunter down toward my son's smaller cabin, fifty yards away.

Spencer, too, is a bear at six in the morning, and isn't open to communication until closer to noon. But he happened to have a cell phone with him. We gave him a call.

"Wake up," I said. "There's a bear coming your way." I could see him moving through the alder, nearing the rear of the cabin.

An eighteen-year old boy is not usually terribly coherent at the crack of dawn. Today, though, the approach of the bear proved an effective wake-up call, and Spencer descended from the cabin's sleeping loft and peered out the enormous picture window—into the big face of the bear.

The bear was less impressed by this guy in the cabin than with the scent of leftover marshmallows and hamburger grease on the ground surrounding Spencer's campfire, and so he busied himself for several minutes sniffing out morsels. Then he trundled off up the hill and melted nonchalantly into the woods.

The encounter lasted all of five minutes, but we were thrilled for days. Every glance out the window became a bear watch; every stump, shadow, or dark log in the woods a potential bruin.

Currently, I am between bears, though I have good reason to feel that the arrival of bear number three is imminent. Laurie, our neighbor up the road, called the other night. A bear that had visited them a couple of times in recent days, and trashed their bird feeders, had just made his third appearance.

"I almost got a photograph of him tonight," she said. "But he slipped away too fast."

Laurie lives a quarter mile away—the bear would be at our place shortly, I hoped, feeling certain that we would be on that night's itinerary. Perhaps, if the Cyr-Nelson theory is correct, this was last year's bear retracing his steps? I got the dogs into the house, put the trash on the bulkhead stairs, and considered walking down to the cabin to alert Spencer. Then I checked the camera for film. All set.

Alas, no bear. The next morning, however, we were awakened at 5:00 a.m. by the sound of one of the cats clawing outside our bedroom window—on the second floor. Mila had climbed the side of our log house. We found Lily, the other cat, perched in the rafters of the front porch. Evidently, they knew that something wilder than they was lurking nearby.

After a few more days of bearless waiting, I decided to go out and explore the woods for a sign: footprints, or foraging, or something. I spent hours slogging through the underbrush with nothing to show for it but mosquito bites and plenty of deer print sightings, but no bear.

And then this morning, as I drove down the dirt road to my office in Brooklin, I had my bear sighting, only it was bear number three sighting me. How could he miss me—I passed within six feet of him, according to Jon, who pulled in right behind me.

"Did you see that bear right behind your car?" Jon said. "I thought it was a dog at first. He must have been about a year old. He waited until you passed by and then crossed the road behind you." No, I did not see the bear. He was shy, but not subtle. They appear when, and where, you least expect it.

This means, of course, that I am still between bears, now awaiting number four.

Time, Tide, and Tuscany

FOR THREE WEEKS ONE JULY, I set my watch by the church bells of San Regolo, Italy. But that is not how you tell time in San Regolo.

The hourly bells chime down its narrow streets, along the stone houses, out over the surrounding olive groves, cypress trees, and vineyards of this tiny village below Castello di Brolio in Tuscany. They give the day sonic texture, but they do not comprise a timetable. Village life is more accurately paced by ripening fruit, weathering stone, and the rhythms of ancient custom. Time is a local phenomenon, not a universal constant.

The succeeding courses of the mid-day meal at the Fabbrizio family's trattoria suggest a typical ancient order: Antipasti, primo piatti, secondo piatti, dolce, caffe. What is not written on the menu, but assumed, is "tempo: lentemente." Leisure. That is to say, a meal must defy haste. Signora Fabbrizio's zuppa di verdure and tortellini are to be savored. One bite at a time. Lentemente. As her husband set the bowl before me, then poured a little olio d'oliva on top, I felt a care and savor in his simple gesture. Like the older man sitting at the table across from me pouring his grappa into his espresso cup. Finale.

Business goes dormant in the early afternoon heat, pacing the day. Even the village clock seems a bit sluggish, resonating languorously in what Billy Collins calls "the swale of the afternoon." The older men and women of the village gather outside the alimentari. They talk, play cards, and watch young Andrea. He explores their pockets and plays with their coins as the old men ask him questions and teach him new words. They are the same villagers who have always gathered in this town square to appreciate this shade, this breeze pushing up the hillside, this company of one another and a young child just learning to talk. Or just to gaze across rows of grape vines. Vintage.

The hillside view from the village square in San Regolo is a medieval vista. Every postage stamp of ground grows a crop: grapes, olives, sunflowers, tomatoes, peaches, plums, and lavender. This earth grows anything. The stone village itself seems to sprout from the hillside as if planted there. In fact, it is the land that is rooted—in community, and community rooted in the land, tendrils of stewardship reaching back a thousand years.

In this old place the narrow cobblestone streets defy haste. Cars are prohibited and prohibitive. A city dating back 1300 years has only had electricity and automobiles for the twinkling of an eye. The ancient Italian city may be wired to the information super highway—an Internet cafe has opened in the shadow of the Duomo in Siena—but to get there you must walk at the pace of the medieval burgher. Lentemente. There is no rushing this settlement.

To the Duomo builders, stone set the pace of building. And my time amidst olive grove and stone village reset my pace to the speed of fruit ripening. Molto bene. Even briefly inhabiting this ancient history has increased my capacity to appreciate the patience and care sewn in each field. It has taken many bells for my thought to ripen thus, afternoons sitting and gazing. No, I cannot be a villager here, but I can temporarily adapt to speeds no greater than ripened thought. Lentemente.

Back home, I start to realize that I too inhabit an old place, though 400 years of European settlement in Castine, Maine, is hardly old to a resident of San Regolo. Yet the Italians would recognize some familiar patterns. Ours is also a community rooted in land, and land rooted in community, a place known for stewardship of forest, bay, and shore, of careful pacing of seaside work, of men and women gathering to sit in the village square of an August afternoon, paced by the speed of melting ice cream cones and creeping elm shade. It is the same young child enjoying attention from the older people.

And the comparison has reminded me of the time required to be familiar enough with a place to feel that sense of community—the intimacy with neighbors and a particular locale that comes only from spending time slowly. It is the neighborhood scale, in an old or new world, that reinforces belonging, the time to take care of a vineyard or grove of trees, the time to conserve the land and the friendships that nourish.

At home, I set my watch to the bells of the Trinitarian church on Main Street, heard throughout town. But I prefer the notion of daily rhythms defined by tide, or lupine blooms, or our ripening tomatoes. Time is a local phenomenon, after all. "Lentemente" is my new standard for "quick" and for community, taking more time to savor our lives.

The Sea Will Hold You

WHO DOESN'T THINK ABOUT BOATS and water activities in the throes of summer?

I resort to my archive of favorite passages and summon the Water Rat from *The Wind in the Willows*. "Believe me, my young friend," says Ratty to Mole, "there is nothing—absolutely nothing—half so much worth doing as simply messing . . . about in boats—or with boats. . . . In or out of 'em, it doesn't matter. Nothing seems to matter, that's the charm of it. Whether you get away, or whether you don't; whether you arrive at your destination or whether you reach somewhere else, or whether you never get anywhere at all, you're always busy, and you never do anything in particular; and when you've done it there's always something else to do, and you can do it if you like, but you'd much better not."

A local author put a much finer point on the pull boat-ward. E.B. White wrote passionately of returning, at the age of seventy, to a childhood pastime. "Whence comes this compulsion to hoist a sail, actually or in a dream?" His first experience, at age four, ended in catastrophe, but instilled an irresistible love-fear relationship. "The sea became my unspoken challenge: the wind, the tide, the fog, the ledge, the bell, the gull that cried help, the never-ending threat and bluff of weather . . . it was as though I had seized hold of a high-tension wire and could not let go." Sailing in local waters—and writing about sailing them—became a new compulsion.

Huck Finn also speaks of boat time versus shore time. Something happens when you're on a raft, just drifting. "You feel mighty free and easy and comfortable on a raft," he says. "Two or three days and nights went by; I reckon I might say they swum by, they slid along so quiet and smooth and lovely." Swum! Perhaps you're a swimmer? Local poet Philip Booth speaks to his daughter as she learns the first lessons of swimming:

> As you float now, where I held you
> and let go, remember when fear
> cramps your heart what I told you:
> lie gently and wide to the light-year
> stars, lie back, and the sea will hold you.

We can all recall that moment of simultaneous terror and exhilaration, when we said, "let go!" and floated free of the adult hands. Suddenly, we discovered our own buoyancy, the support that was simply *there* all along, and we paddled toward free agency. It works for writing too. The words and sentences are there; the models are there; the ideas, experiences, inspiration will float you and your boat. There is nothing half so worth doing as . . . telling your story, setting forth upon the waves of imagination, letting your sails luff a little, drift, or haul the sail in tight and dip the rail to the water. Every sentence has its own hull shape, keel and jib size. Keep a hand on the tiller and bring us to the mooring. Lie back, and your words will hold you . . . actually, or in a dream.

The Migration

TIME WAS, AUGUST MEANT DEPARTURE. Our annual Maine sojourn ended at TSA, flying "home" to Chicago. We disembarked from summer itself at the curb and trudged into the terminal. The migration back to where we came from was saturated with melancholy. We dutifully emptied our pockets of sand and the emotional savor of our summer lives, placed memories in a safe place in the checked luggage, dragged our sadness down the ramp to September and the resumption of our "real" lives.

Or, some years, we took the slow route home, driving a jam-packed minivan—three kids, two dogs, sundry bicycles and strollers, and all our beachcombing treasure—heading down the Maine turnpike to Boston. Are we there yet? No. And even after arrival, we were reluctant to actually be "there" yet.

Which was the real life—the all too short stint in Maine, or the remainder of the year in the exile we called normal life?

Each migration started with sorting. What positively *must* come back with us? A few carefully chosen stones from the beach (considered for karat and character), some shards of pottery; a few shells, clay pipe, and glass bottle neck washed up on the collecting shore? There is usually a new maritime chart or Ordinance Survey map, sundry postcards, new books from the local store, perhaps a commemorative hat—Big Ernie's Castine

Variety. Birch bark. Driftwood. These won't take up mini-van space nor precious luggage weight limits.

Call it vacation triage. What are this summer's sacred objects, talismans of time spent away from routine, that must not be left behind. And what *can* be left behind for rediscovery next summer? What should be tossed back into the sea and trusted to future beachcombers? Difficult decisions. We cleave to our treasures. After all, summer is about collecting, literally and fig-uratively. Years worth of summer jars of sand, heart and circle rocks, sit on my shelves even now.

We collect ephemeral moments too, and they are easily packed and retrieved. The shiver of a fish on the line or the sound of the paddle against the gunwale traversing the pond—Quiet! Don't spook the fish, or the loons. Summer trains our senses to absorb and archive the minutiae of any walk through the woods, of every ice cream cone on the dock, of sunsets, of thundershowers rollicking across the bay.

Oh, to be in Chicago now that summer's there—No! Our home thoughts from abroad are the inverse. We know it's muggy and hot—again—while here on the coast we will have a fire in the fireplace and consume the daily batch of blueberry muffins. Blueberries will not make it through security and far be it from us to surrender them. We know exactly what to do: bake, then consume the last quarts of this year's careful picking.

In August, the dreaded "lasts" commence: one more snooze in the hammock, a last walk down to the dock to inventory boats, a final trip to the library to return our summer reading, another pie, another muffin. The tide comes in once more, goes out once more. The tide of summer goes out. Departure is a grieving/binge-baking process.

Time was, when we arrived home, the inventory continued. There are the summer tan lines, new freckles, and growth to measure and appreciate. Stature too. Each summer away has accomplishments: a new swimming skill or distance, fish landed (size and number), paddling prowess, and pebble jar. Somehow, the transitions between home and away highlight accomplishments. Both places are a comparative background to evolution, even for the grown-ups. Maine doesn't leave you as it found you. In my case, there was always fresh writing inspiration. Canned for the winter, summer thoughts fed my creativity in the cold months away.

Time was, my heart sank as our minivan crested the final hill on route 93 southbound and the metropolis came into view. We were back to the tall buildings, the haze, the concrete, the grid-lock, the other migratory beings fighting to swim upstream back to jobs and schools and life on the clock. Or were we swimming downstream? Were we returning from our spawning grounds of summer spent in the generational headwaters of our family—the creativity and languor zone—recharged and ready for a new season back in the big salt pond of suburbia?

Like the forest that wants to reclaim cleared land, our off-summer lives wanted us back. We preferred our summer fields. We strove to keep them open. How did we finally cope, transiting the equinoxes of Maine life and life anywhere else? We stopped being bi-polar. We stopped being migratory beings. We stayed in Maine.

Autumn

Season of Mists

THE BRISK WIND OFF THE BAY has a whiff of change—the timing between summer and autumn can catch you off-guard. The maple leaves are not yet turning, the acorns and apples are still plumping on the branch, but there is a palpable tipping point and the onset of an autumnal rhythm. The farmers have cut and baled their hay—perhaps two cuttings—and tucked it in the barn. My lawn clamors for a final pass with the mower. Or, let it go? It won't grow for much longer. But is the woodpile sufficient for a whole winter's heat? That's the tipping point: ripening versus retreat to hibernation. I'm in no hurry to be mounting the studded snow tires.

There is a certain kind of day, however, when you sense that you've reached the seasonal outer buoy—when the next tack had better be down the reach, under a small jib, toward home and snug harbor.

Are we *there* yet?

To John Keats, autumn contained a second harvest and plentiful blossoming—"mellow fruitfulness," he called it—to the discerning eye, not just a *segue* to winter or the shutdown of summer. Autumn, Keats says, is for gleaners, those blueberry pickers who find the sweetest midnight-blue fruit from around the granite outcroppings, like bears storing up for the winter.

Keats was a gleaner, too—not so much of what was actually *there*, as what he *felt* about what was there. Keats gleaned poems from his own ripeness for inspiration, growth, and beauty. His autumn of bounty was as much an interior season as it was the mellowing of the English countryside.

Poets are society's gleaners, scooping up thoughtful morsels left in the furrow after the haste of more prosaic harvesters. You need to walk slowly and look carefully to see fruit in unexpected places.

I detect a few lingering feelings of the season just past. I want to be a gleaner of summer, not autumn. I haven't fully appreciated the thoughts and rhythms of summer. That outer buoy marks a further channel to navigate—to open communications with oneself and sail into romantic waters.

Alas, there are too many choppy currents that throng what we allow for slack time—a compulsion to be going, doing, making—as if only outward industry is achievement. Because it is the season to pause, summer confronts us with the interstices of life. Time elongates, allowing us to see pockets of thought that were blurred as we trotted briskly past. Gazing too far in the distance makes us steer as the crow flies. By meandering we savor the subtleties of our progress: the perfume of spruce, the grasshoppers in the tomato plants, the crows caucusing in the white pines, the perfect webs the spiders are knitting in the grasses.

And Keats would approve of my hammock under the oaks. "Mowing can wait," he would say. Tomorrow morning—make wild blueberry muffins. Soon enough we will make time for apple picking. But in a hammock, this late summer/early autumn evening, Keats and I can just listen to the "gathering swallows twitter in the skies."

Emptying the Harbor

LAST FRIDAY, RIGHT ON SCHEDULE, the floating town docks were hoisted out of the water with a crane and stacked in the municipal parking lot, their storage space for the winter. Our platform for mackerel fishing is gone; the red and white "20 Minute Tie-Up" sign is sentinel to nothing. The harbor seals venture closer as the human activity withdraws. The yacht club long ago stopped firing the cannon at the official moment of sunset. As if we'd turned back the clocks early on Halloween weekend, we have recalibrated for the impending season beside a winter ocean. We are reefed.

The docks will rest until April, the barnacles, algae, and sea-weed gradually release their hold, shedding onto the macadam to stink on a warm day in January. The Breeze, the town's takeout food stand, has also closed for the winter, though its menu under the awning still advertises crab rolls, fried clams, and soft-serve ice cream, staples for summer visitors and hovering seagulls. This storing of the docks is the final phase of a ritual preparation for winter—freezing weather, flowing ice, and punishing Nor'eas-ters that will sweep up the bay. As people begin to wrap their houses, skirt the foundations with plastic sheeting, stack the firewood close to the ell, and call the man about snowplowing, the harbor, too, must hunker down. We are on the verge of the season in which it is weather's turn to impose. It is the season of storage, of firesides, of interior work, and of waiting.

Kenny Eaton, whose father, Alonzo, and grandfather, Mace, ran the adjacent boatyard before him, has been hauling boats out of the water for weeks . . . or generations. The landside of the boatyard fills with sailboats standing on their keels, braced by stanchions, to be power washed and then shrink-wrapped for hibernation. The weathered shingles of Eaton's, the steady retreat of equipment to the sheds amidst the culch of boat servicing, the abatement of dockside activity, like the shortening days, herald yachting's torpor. When you can see the propeller, rudder, and keel of a sleek sailboat, its charm is fled: the ungainly innards of its trick of flying before the wind has been exposed. The boat becomes an object of maintenance and not a fleet craft.

Eaton's yard isn't large and fills quickly, so the larger boats must be taken by trailer right out of town. Like a parade of nautical floats, mastless ketches and sloops, bulky cabin cruisers, and muscular work boats all slip up Main Street by the Trinitarian church on their way up the hill and out of town. Scant spectators stop and peer as Kenny tows them to his upland winter harbor for storage or repairs: a massive quonset hut next to a peat bog, ten miles from the harbor, where the maintenance work of winter can proceed out of the weather, in the woods. The engines' vital fluids will be drained, the hulls scraped and caulked, sanded and painted, rigging retooled, remounted, revived. The wooden boats come up for air, dry and shrink, the fiberglass boats shed algae. Gallons of marine varnish are brushed into teak and mahogany decking, extending the usefulness of wood plying corrosive saltwater. Even Kenny says, "why would anyone want to get involved with a boat."

At the shore, the boatyard is now a forlorn collection of white rubber globes, buoys stenciled with the names of boat owners. They bob on the tide, but without their boat to turn its bow into the current they give no telltale sign of the direction of flow. A forest of masts during the summer, the harbor is now a field of these buoy "erratics," vacant between the town dock and Smith's Cove and Brooksville. Nothing much interrupts flat water, skerries, and white caps except a channel marker. Nothing interrupts our inspection of the farms and forest on the opposite shore. All the leaves are down; buildings emerge from their summer cover. The hillsides are mizzened by maples and oaks. Nothing interrupts the perception of distance. There is no longer a middle ground in this picture.

But for a lone lobsterman, whose catch has not yet migrated farther out into the bay, the human boating presence on the water recedes, a tide of activity that will be out until the spring equinox, when the migratory process is reversed. Kenny will haul the boats back down to the water and re-insert them, following some improvised sequence, parading back from bog side to harbor side. Freshly painted, newly engineered, ready for rigging, one by one, the boats will float back to their globes to be tethered. The docks will be dropped back in place at the town dock and patrons of the Breeze will flock back like the seagulls at around the time "lilacs in the dooryard bloom." And the 20-minute tie-ups resume.

Sailing Back in Time

LAST WEEK, I SPENT A MORNING in the 19th century.

I shipped out on a wooden schooner named the *Bowdoin*, as if entering a time machine, sailing across Penobscot Bay from Searsport to Castine with fifteen high school juniors from Belfast. They were students in an American Studies course who were learning about the Age of Sail.

Wearing their varsity football jackets and jeans, they seemed like anything but a schooner crew from the 1800s. Some of them had never been in a sailboat, though they had grown up by the sea in a town with a proud shipping tradition. But on this day, they hoisted sail—up the *Bowdoin*'s two gaff-rigged masts as First Mate Heather Stone commanded, "Give way on the peak and throat together. Heave! Heave!"

They learned to coil rope in the proper manner; they tied new knots, making lines fast; they charted and steered a course; and they calculated nautical miles and speed the old-fashioned way. This was all state-of-the-art seamanship for the 1800s—the roots of maritime skills that remain fundamental to modern shipping. Or even space travel—astronauts use nautical terms for their physical orientation in space.

I listened to the creak of the wooden rigging and canvas sails, the gentle wash of waves on the bow, the easy listing of an old wooden hull, and the sound of free fuel—wind. And I appreciated the tactile effects of my grandfather's grandfather's time— the feel of weathered rope on my hands, of fog on my face, of muscles I'm unaccustomed to using simply to transit eight miles of saltwater, to squeeze seven knots out of a wooden hull, parsing the bay.

It had the feel of inhabiting history, not just reading about it, the difference between information and experience. This was not a documentary observed—it was observation documented.

As I stood amidships surveying Penobscot Bay, I imagined a day, not so long ago, when a fleet of such schooners might have plied these waters within view of the lookout of this very schooner. The last voyage of a commercial sailing vessel carrying cargo down the Bagaduce River and into Penobscot Bay is still within living memory of a few folks living at these waters' edge.

The captain, Eliot Rappaport, offered an intriguing perspective. Schooners were the tractor-trailer trucks of their day. It's only in the last century that we've gotten an infrastructure of roads and overland transport. Eighty years ago, the way to get your goods from point A to B was by sea.

The *Bowdoin*, I learned, was built 100 years ago, down the coast a bit. It is designed for arctic exploration. Ice will squeeze its hull like an orange seed, raising it out of harm's crushing way in a deep freeze north of 70 degrees latitude. It was built to be handled by small crews—cheap to build, cheap to run, typical of the fishing schooners of the Age of Sail . . . a hard-working vehicle as well as a beautiful vessel, hardly an artifact, sailing past Turtle Head on a fall day.

On a 19th-century fall morning, schooners laden with bricks would be coming down the Bagaduce River from the brickyards on the shore of the Northern Bay, exporting the very clay soil to Boston or Philadelphia builders.

Other schooners, carrying lime, granite, or sardines up and down the Eastern Seaboard, would be tacking between Turtle Head and Cape Rosier. The bay would be alive with masts and trimmed sails—signs of commerce, rather than the present era's sailing for leisure.

On a 19th-century morning, when Bangor was the lumber capital of the world and steam was not yet a cost-effective nautical technology, this bay might have felt very different. And part of the American experience might have been seventeen-year-olds from Belfast, already with a few years before the mast, on their way to a life at sea—perhaps preparing to command a huge Down Easter of their own, outbound from Searsport for blue water, sailing for the exotic ports of the world.

On a 19th-century morning, Searsport would have been the nexus of shipbuilders and sea captains, some of whom spent years away from home on a single voyage. At times, it took three months just to pass 'round Cape Horn. They sailed with their families on long, lonely reaches from Down East Maine to ports of call at the ends of the earth, sailing wheat, iron, steel, or 500,000 gallons of case oil to Hong Kong.

They brought ice to India and the West Indies. These captains sailed home with firecrackers, feathers, matting, tungsten ore, silk, tea, exotic artwork, and home furnishings filling their holds. And they imported glimmers of new understanding of peoples and places from the profoundly different cultures they experienced.

After my morning in the 19th century, I can imagine trading my varsity-letter jacket for a few more days under sail in a wooden schooner . . . and perhaps the chance to sail a Down Easter full of fabulous ice to a tropical island. I could trade what would be a new concept—cold—for glimmers of some new, tropical understanding.

Photo Days

THE SUNLIGHT IN THE OLD PHOTO looks as it does today on an early autumn afternoon. The facade of the white clapboard school shines, and the shadows cling to the posed figures, the shade line close to where we would see it now, more than 130 years later.

There is even a familiar casualness and relaxed demeanor to this group of teachers and students gathered in Castine for the Adams School photo circa 1875.

The two boys in the third-floor window project a surprisingly jaunty posture, although it must have been a little harrowing perching way up there. I've stood in that window. Perhaps they were assigned the task of ringing the bell in the cupola, the same bell that we still ring on the first and last days of school.

And that shadowy man in the stovepipe hat! Who was he? The principal? How stiff and dour.

As all-school photo day comes around again, I am looking at this gilt-framed photograph that hangs in the front hall of the Adams School, of which I'm the current principal. I like to imagine that it was taken on photo day, and that the Adams corps has been herded to the front steps—and windows and doors—to stand still, smile, and peer into the camera . . . and the future. They seem somewhat less practiced at taking part in group photos. It must have been a rare occasion. Little did they know they were gazing at us.

Today, the wide-brimmed felt hats on the boys and the stove-pipe hats on the men would be replaced by baseball caps. Today, we don't see many dresses and petticoats, vests, long suit coats, and ties during school hours either. Fashion changes.

Yet today's students and teachers probably have much in common with those in 1875. We live on their land, in their houses, and attend their school as the heirs and stewards of this place. Too bad we weren't able to see them in their Halloween costumes!

I wonder . . . what were the hot-button town issues of the day—parking downtown, as it is now? Or perhaps horse manure? The price of fuel? No, that was the era of schooners and Maine-built Down Easters. Who did they vote for: Ulysses Grant in 1872, Rutherford Hayes in 1876? I wonder if any of the adults in the old photo actually heard Lincoln's voice at Gettysburg. Certainly, they were all present at the dedication of the Civil War monument on the common just across from the school.

It's tempting to want to peer beyond the frame of the old photo, to see the neighboring houses, the schoolyard, or the interior of the old building that feels so familiar to us. Adams School has been in continuous operation since 1854.

Old photos convey a rich sense of place, of a certain conscious-ness of one's sense of self, and of one's relationship to the imme-diate group, to time, and, most important, to community.

But we tend to forget the future community at whom we gaze in the casual immediacy of our present sense of "frame." Actu-ally, history is our frame, and it's interesting to peer around its edges.

Tomorrow we will herd the current group of teachers and stu-dents onto the same steps. In some latter-day Castine, the future town will inspect us, our shade, our nonchalance, our coats and ties and hats. (However, they won't see boys in the attic window!)

"Who were they?" they'll wonder, looking at 54 students and their teachers way back then. "What were they like?" they'll ask as they review the old yearbooks or wonder at the old town reports and a school and town budget that seems a pittance by their contemporary standards.

What was that young boy in the front row thinking as he mugged for the camera? And what was the girl in the second row whispering to her neighbor? Why is that kid holding a giant zucchini? In photos of the whole student body, there is always a shy girl, a brash boy, a distracting, errant curl, an untimely gust, a nudge, a comment just too good to wait. "Smile! Cheese?" Click. Frame it.

Those residents of the future will live on our land, in our houses, and attend our school as the heirs and stewards of this place and this sunlight. Too bad they won't be able to see us in our Halloween costumes—nor we see theirs.

Things change—and nothing changes. The light will, presumably, feel familiar. And, I hope, the same bell will ring in the cupola—the same bell that rang in 1875.

Testing a String Theory

Joey Spinazola has been saving string—a lot of string. He started in the summer when a character from his favorite television program, *Family Matters*, gave him an idea. "Steve Erkel invented a time machine, and something went wrong with it. The insides looked like a huge ball of string. I thought, 'That would be cool to make.'"

Joey started winding yarn procured from his sisters, and eventually one of his father's t-shirts (cut into strips), until he had created the basketball-sized, tightly wound, "magical ball of fame." It came to school and had been sitting in his cubby since October. And then, one Monday, it seemed like a good time to determine just how much string it contained. "I think it might reach all the way to Eaton's," Joey said. "Maybe to the water." Anything farther than that would exceed expectations and be a triumph. A local string theory had been born, and it required testing.

It's probably possible to estimate the length of the MBF through a few simple equations using the diameter of the string ball and the varying thickness of the string and yarn wound around it, to know if it would go the distance to Eaton's—or anywhere else in town. But when it's a sunny, warm day in November—a gift before winter's onset—and there's a cohort of willing scientists, a gravitational pull downhill toward the harbor, and still fifteen minutes before the recess bell rings and classes resume, a physical test of theories is irresistible. And a test would achieve a determination, not just an estimate.

With a nod to his physicist forebears and the help of Brianne sitting on the school steps and holding fast to the bitter end, Joey took the ball and gave it a big kick, sending it rolling toward the library.

Theory number one: a humongous string ball given a kick on a slope will keep on rolling until acted upon by another force. Or, as Newton wrote, "A body persists in a state of rest or of uniform motion unless acted upon by an external force." False. Joey's ball rolled exactly three maple trees down School Street and then stopped. It needed another application of external force (a second kick). But there was no apparent force acting upon it that would explain why it didn't stay in motion. Inertia and entropy are hard to see. Clearly, one of two things was going on: this ball simply did not wish to be unwound, or the second law of Spinazola String Theory is in effect. It is the Anti-winding Force. This has sometimes been called the silent force, which physicists have struggled to decipher for years. It explains everything from the unraveling of sweaters (PRP: Perl Retrograde Phenomenon) to fishing knot intransigence (LTE: Line Torpor Effect). Joey persuaded the MBF to keep moving.

It did. When it reached the bottom of Green Street, and even turned the corner, the whole cohort was elated.

Theory number two: a humongous string ball comprised of several different weights of string will roll at a different rate for each weight. That is, cotton fabric "string" will roll faster than fluffy pink yarn. Or, as Newton put it, "Force equals mass times acceleration (F = ma): the net force on an object is equal to the mass of the object multiplied by its acceleration." This is false, according to Spinazola String Theory. It makes no difference who is throwing or kicking, or which gauge of string is coming off the ball, a string ball will take its own sweet time, going uphill or down—it makes no difference. MBFs have a mind all their own.

Theory number three: Joey's ball is large enough to reach Eaton's before running out. True. Joey's ball was more than large enough to reach Eaton's. In fact, it was more than large enough to turn the corner at the Variety store and keep on going, as Elizabeth and Harry Kaiserian are our witnesses. The string ball, after pausing on the steps of the Variety for a documentary photo, kept right on going—past the bookstore, gallery, Saltmeadow Properties, and the Water Witch.

On Wednesday, Joey ruminated on the best and worst part of the experience. "Nice walk! Having other kids unroll it was nice," he said. "Tangles were annoying. And I thought it would go faster. The knots slowed it down; made it bounce too much."

And so to the Adams School Annals of Science we have added a new test of velocity, acceleration, mass, and propulsion: the MBF. And to feet, yards, meters, astronomical units, leagues, fathoms, hectares, cubits, and spans, we add the Magical Ball of Fame, a unit of measurement to be forever defined as the distance from the Adams School front stairs to the northwest edge of the white building just uphill from the old Saltmeadow building, clockwise, via Green, Water, and Main streets. Joey figures it's also the equivalent of one circumference of the MMA football field (OCMMAFF). But it's easier to just say, "It's about one MBF from here." It's sure to catch on. Check Wikipedia.

The Memory
of This Place

"THE LAND WAS OURS BEFORE WE WERE THE LAND'S"—or so it felt, back in December, the first time we walked the property that we now call "our land." As Lesley and I traipsed through the light snow, down the faint dirt road and into a clearing in a grove of cedar trees, it felt familiar, as if we already inhabited it.

"This is beautiful," we said. "This feels like ours."

Two months after buying the land, we had yet to see it without a covering of snow, which was deeper following February's succession of nor'easters. This deep snowpack co-opted the usual process of getting acquainted. We spent many a winter afternoon wallowing in the newly fallen thigh-deep snow or playing follow the leader in one another's footprints in order to keep from wallowing, while exploring our 21 wooded acres. The light, the wind, and the woodland sounds we sampled at all times of day, confirmed that we were witnesses to hibernation. Our land was asleep.

Every visit was a test of our Thoreauvian appreciation for winter's vestments and our land's embrace of ice, snow, and a certain slant of light through the evergreens. Sometimes we just perched on a log in a sunny patch to watch and listen. While most plant and animal species are far from wakening in their burrow or seedpod torpor, tree activity abounded. The crisp creaking of stiff upper branches, purling together on a gusty afternoon, emerged, distinct from the background chorus of waving Aeolian boughs. We began to discern the exact source of deeper, sonorous cracks and groans emanating from half-fallen spruce, or the staccato clicking of birches rimed with ice. The trees spoke to us in their individual dialects. On our last visit, we discovered the brook. The cleft that meandered from North to South below a hill was running with the onset of spring thaw. We added "babbling" to the voices of our land.

One advantage to this winter reconnoitering was the ease of tracking woodland denizens. We had yet to *see* a deer on our land, but their footprints and grazing marks on the cedar trees suggested a robust herd camping in various patches of moss and ferns. We could tell that they were large, medium, and small, and our dog, Gus, delighted in tracking their movements back and forth through the shallower snow in the thickly grown groves. By following their tracks, we learned to adopt their pathfinding strategies in snow. The deer know how not to wallow.

A murder of impertinent crows loved to make its surveillance known. Hopping jauntily from branch to branch, casually taking in our progress up the hill at the back of our rectangular lot, they called one to another, alerting their fellow wild tenants of our whereabouts. They brokered our visits.

We had yet to see the enormous woodpeckers, which drill deep holes into the expired pine trees, making gargantuan wooden flutes. Other nests abounded for our inspection, wedged in leafless branches, abandoned, awaiting the return of songbird tenants next month. Gus sniffed out the nest of the grouse. It blurred into flight and spooked the big retriever every time. It occurred to me that his experience of the land was primarily olfactory: he knew wild wood beasts lived there, but he was not yet able to link scent with appearance. We constantly hoped for the appearance of something wild without benefit of a whiff to validate the expectation.

Though we now owned the land in a legal sense, we were clearly nothing more than the most recent in a long line of caretakers. Its prior human owners could be traced back to the earliest days of European settlement, but those records simply fall within the lifetime of a few of the oldest trees. The trees themselves narrated the encyclopedic story of former loggers, farmers, even orchardists. The stone walls, just poking through the March thaw, continued telling an age-old story of cultivation and field clearing. But it was the singular car-sized boulder, probably a glacial erratic, settled a few yards from where we would eventually build our house, that reminded us of the longest memory inhabiting these acres: the deep memory of stone.

And so, when we spotted the big owl, after weeks of tracking walks and intimations of our wild co-inhabitants, it felt like a sign: the woods responding to our application for permanent resident status. Any aspiring Thoreauvian knows that the owls are the ombudsmen for any given sylvan glade. Minerva sat watching us serenely from a low branch of a maple tree, startling us with the directness of her gaze. Owls have a very human visage. They look you full in the face without the least bit of timidity or shyness. They meet your gaze. We felt honored.

Who knew for how many weeks she had been observing us before deciding that we could be trusted with the knowledge of her presence? The woods had spoken. The owl now knew we knew she knew. And on every walk in the woods we were expectant of an owl sighting.

As an act of good faith and reciprocity, I made seven birdhouses and attached them to trees growing on the edge of the clearing. I planned to make another fit for an owl, a bespoke birdhouse, now that I knew Minerva's size. It would be my way of speaking back to the woods and accepting my role as caretaker, happy to play my part in the memory of this place, happy to be a denizen, happy to *be* "the land's."

Timorous Beasties and Woodpile Thermodynamics

IT WAS TIME—the log pile in the driveway had seasoned and dried all summer and was ready to be stored away, brought under cover and nearer the woodstove for heat in the winter months ahead.

As Thoreau says of his firewood stumps in *Walden*, "They warmed me twice—once while I was splitting them, and again when they were on the fire." My wood came luxuriously cut and split this year, so stacking and moving and restacking was my only collateral heat. And heat when it was least needed, in a mild autumn—"hotumn," as it was called. If the weather didn't yet augur winter, the calendar did. "An' bleak December's winds ensuin, Baith snell an' keen!" as Robert Burns put it. "Snell" is fairly onomatopoeic—bitter. Transcendentalists and Scottish poets are very focused on the man-heat-weather-vocabulary continuum.

As the layers of firewood were stacked in the garage, log by log, armful by armful, it was clear they had been inhabited and renovated between May and October by several families of mice. There were nests of moss and leaves, storehouses of acorns, and even a privy. The beasties clearly had intentions of winter-long occupancy. I hated to thwart their plans. Apparently, my fuel was also another creature's heat. One critter's heat is another critter's condominium.

> *Thou saw the fields laid bare an' waste,*
> *An' weary winter comin' fast,*
> *An' cozie here, beneath the blast,*
> *Thou thought to dwell—*
> *Till crash! the cruel coulter past*
> *Out thro' thy cell.*

Furthermore, one man's Subaru Outback cabin air filter is another critter's food pantry, evidently. The gnawed acorns stashed under my hood were a source of great amusement at my autumn service appointment. "Try dryer sheets," said the service manager. "Or moth balls." Just for good measure, I poured a box of moth balls into the wood pile, once I had it tightly stashed in the garage. Take that, ye timorous beasties. After all, I too was nesting and, while sympathetic, was not in a sharing mood.

Burns was looking over my shoulder again. He addressed a similar situation while mowing, turning out a mouse nest and pondering the effect and addressing the affected.

> *Wee, sleekit, cow'rin, tim'rous beastie,*
> *O, what a panic's in thy breastie!*
> *Thou need na start awa sae hasty,*
> *Wi' bickering brattle!*
> *I wad be laith to rin an' chase thee,*
> *Wi' murd'ring pattle!*

For every action there is an equal and opposite reaction. But whose was the action and whose the *re*action? Was the ball in my court? Was I imposer or imposed upon? There was invasive action going on in the basement now and I had to defend the perimeter of my nest. No good having cute timorous beasties nibbling the wiring and bedding in my insulation. I stanched the incursion with extreme prejudice—murd'ring pattle. Until I came face to face with the mouse in the photo box. My, didn't he look comfy. And just where had he gotten all that angora yarn? Acorns galore in a draft-free *pied á terre*! Timorous beastie, or invasive species?

The poet, as usual, was ahead of us both. "The best-laid schemes o' mice an' men/ Gang aft agley," Burns wrote. I am indeed agley. Mr. Wee Sleekit seems less agley than me. We'll see how he feels about returning to his lodging back in the field. Tell your friends, wee mouse! Awa wi' ye!

Did that door just lock shut behind me? Wee mouse! Let me back in! It's *snell* an *keen* out here!

Afterword

SAYING IT

WHY WRITE? For a long time, I didn't understand why it felt so important to write down words. I just did it. Having journalists as parents might be considered a powerful influence. My high school English teacher, Mr. Walker, advocated writing about one's experience, like his hero Thoreau who would wander the woods or sit beside Walden Pond and observe. Noticing the way things are, the way things happen, the way things feel deserves expression. It's good to say why things matter. "How much we are the woods we wander in," says Richard Wilbur.

The typewriter itself is an influence. When I was a kid, the sound of writing broke the silence of the house at bedtime. Stopping and starting, the typewriter carriage sliding back and forth like a trolley, the song of text being hammered on paper proceeded out of silence from the industrial-sized Royal type. Writing, Dad was explaining via his percussive typing, was something you worked at, tried and retried, and then polished. It was important to say things clearly, simply, directly. He was a print journalist. And he probably wasn't aware of what he was modeling, just trying to meet deadline.

Later mentors made it obvious that by trying to say things you clarify your thoughts. Writing is thinking in plain sight. For instance, it charged my fourth-grade storytelling with the effort to be correct, clear, and stylish. Mr. Pratt wouldn't let me get away with clichés in 11th and 12th grade; he challenged every word to earn its place in a sentence. And I also wanted to type—as fast as Dad. Furthermore, stories written on a typewriter had more authority because they looked like *real* writing. If you justify the margins, you justify the rhetoric. Not. I still got points off for misspellings and punctuation. Writing is never done. "A poem is never finished," says W.H. Auden, "only abandoned." My favorite poem, "Fern Hill," went through some 89 drafts before Dylan Thomas "abandoned" it. I wonder if he typed?

As Dad wrote newspaper stories or worked on his books after work, soft light from the gooseneck lamp arching over the keyboard seemed to pool around his concentration. I recall the poise of his hands above the home keys, as he awaited the next phrase or sentence and the next flurry of prose. The cadence of his certain thoughts punctuated summer twilight. It melded with the sprinklers and cicadas outside in suburban Chicago, every ten or fifteen words the typewriter's little bell sending the carriage zippering back to drag a new line across the page from the margin. I had to wonder: What was he noticing? What was he trying to *say?* Saying it goes beyond journalism, various poets taught me.

There are many Phillip Booth poems that are among my favorites: "Eaton's Boatyard," "First Lesson." They are rooted in a place that I love, an experience that I connect with, or a definition that seems right, precise, and essential to being a father, a husband, a writer, a resident of a certain locale. In "Strip," Booth draws an existential lesson from Mobius, and the simple path of a piece of paper that has only one side. It talks about a man turning into himself, and I read it for the first time after my father died.

Another Booth poem, "Saying It," has always defined something about the core of writing and feels like essential reading for us all. It's the best poem I know for expressing how hard and important it is to notice and then choose and then use words. On discovery, it felt as if Booth's words explained myself, to myself—finally. In "Saying It," he talks about that elemental motive to find a word that is worth listening to, that justifies its place in the sentence, however tentative or halting. Why write? He says why. The poem begins:

> *Saying it. Trying*
> *to say it. Not*
> *to answer to*
>
> *logic, but leaving*
> *our very lives open*
> *to how we have*
>
> *to hear ourselves*
> *say what we mean.*

Of course! It's not just saying it, but listening to ourselves as we say it. We are each our own audience, *and* the speaker. We are the meaning we mean to share. Looking for the right words is looking for definition, trying to refine one's expression in word and deed as a way of looking, seeing, and acting. Saying it is feeling, then doing, and then sharing. Saying it is loving something outside of oneself. Saying it is measuring and defining oneself. Saying it is the song of oneself. Saying it, finally, is trying to be certain that your life is *about* something.

The poem ends:

> *We wake, at night, to*
>
> *imagine, and again wake*
> *at dawn to begin: to let*
> *the intervals speak*
>
> *for themselves, to*
> *listen to how they*
> *feel, to give pause*
>
> *to what we're about:*
> *to relate ourselves,*
> *over and over; in*
>
> *time beyond time*
> *to speak some measure*
> *of how we hear the music:*
>
> *today if ever to*
> *say the joy of trying*
> *to say the joy.*

There. I can't say it better than that, at least on this draft. Thank goodness for poets.

About the Author

Author portrait © Michelle L. Morby

Sometimes, I just "take a line out for a walk," as Paul Klee says about his drawing process. Mine are lines of words drawing figures of life here in Maine: the wind on the knoll out back of the house, interstices of land and water, critters and neighbors. Maine is my state of mind, regardless where I'm sitting down to write.

After 35 years teaching and administrating in public and private schools in Boston, San Francisco, Chicago, Philadelphia, and Castine, Maine, **Todd Nelson** retired to write and bake bread and the scones of destiny. His writing has appeared in a number of newspapers and periodicals, including *Ellsworth American, Castine Patriot, Maine Boats, Homes & Harbors, Bangor Daily News, Maine Times, Philadelphia Inquirer, Taproot, Christian*

Science Monitor, Wooden Boat, Northern Journeys, and *Portland Press Herald.* He lives with his wife, Lesley, and with their grand dogs, Betty and Lola, in Penobscot, Maine.

Ariel Rose Nelson moved to Castine with her parents and siblings in 1998 when she was in fifth grade. She is a graduate of Adams School in Castine and George Stevens Academy in Blue Hill. One thing led to another. She received her BFA from Glasgow School of Art and her MFA from Gray's School of Art at Robert Gordon University, Aberdeen. She is a free-lance illustrator and artist. Her favorite tree is the old oak in Arthur Wardwell's field above Hatch Cove.